What people are saying about …

Love Life Again

"Wow! Yes! Tracie Miles shines her flashlight into the dark cave, and she welcomes us to walk back into the light."

—**Tricia Lott Williford**, author of *And Life Comes Back* and *You Can Do This*

"I know a book is going to be really good when, by chapter 1, I've started making a mental list of all of the people who need to read it. If I knew you, you'd be on the list. Short story: read this book because it's more than a book. It's a key that unlocks the door to the life you were made for."

—**Jennifer Dukes Lee**, author of *It's All Under Control* and *The Happiness Dare*

"When there's a big difference between what you *expect* in life and what you *get* in life, disappointment, discouragement, and even despair can overwhelm you. In *Love Life Again*, Tracie reaches out as a compassionate and candid friend, opening her heart, sharing her own experiences, and offering Christ-centered tools to help you choose new ways to truly love your one-and-only life."

—**Cheri Gregory**, coauthor of *Overwhelmed: How to Quiet the Chaos and Restore Your Sanity*

"When I got a copy of this book, I read it cover to cover in one sitting. It was exactly what my heart needed. In *Love Life Again*, Tracie openly shares her life struggles in a way that you know she understands the pain of disappointment. Her depth of faith, mixed with practical ways to move forward with joy, will inspire you to love your life again! This is a great life-transforming book!"

—**Courtney Joseph**, writer at
WomenLivingWell.org, the home
of Good Morning Girls

"We've all experienced it. A difficult season in life when struggles are plentiful, joy is fleeting, and hope seems just outside our reach. That's why I'm so excited about Tracie Miles's newest book, *Love Life Again*. It's overflowing with encouragement, truth, and practical tips to help shift our thinking in a positive direction. Each chapter is filled with rich insights that will lighten your soul and ignite hope in your heart again. Tracie reminds us all that we're not on this earth to simply survive. We're here to thrive and live an abundant life through Christ … today and every day."

—**Leah DiPascal**, speaker, writer for
First 5 App, Proverbs 31 Ministries

"Traci Miles, in her new book, *Love Life Again: Finding Joy When Life Is Hard*, provides invaluable insight navigating through real-life challenges. With great clarity, focus, and inspiration, she takes the reader into the depths of hope that will encourage even those going through the most difficult circumstances. Get this book. You will find joy as an anchor and begin to experience all the love this life has to offer."

—**Robin Bertram**, author of *No Regrets*,
speaker, vice president of Media Relations,
Christian Women in Media Association

"Practical, doable steps to help us move toward loving our lives … the ones we actually have right now, that is what *Love Life Again* gives us. Tracie has and is living this message. So whether you are in the throes of painful blows you never expected to experience or simply stuck in the mundane, day-to-day life demands, Tracie's book helps us to have the lives we want, even if and even when nothing ever changes."

—**Lynn Cowell**, author of *Make Your Move*

"With compassion and clarity, Tracie shares her journey from a place of deep loss to a place of love and laughter, peace and purpose. More than a message, *Love Life Again* is an invitation to journey toward hope. When the life you once dreamed of feels more like a forever-gone reality than a hope-filled possibility, Tracie comes alongside every one of us, not only with practical steps we can take, but also with words of hope and healing—the kind found only in Christ our Healer."

—**Denise J. Hughes**, author of *Deeper Waters*
and the *Word Writers* Bible Study series

"With just the right blend of grit and grace, Tracie invites us to stop waiting for the life we want and start loving the life we've got. Packed with rich biblical wisdom, vulnerable personal stories, and inspiring insight, this beautiful book reminds us that life may not be perfect, but it is precious. A must-read for all of us who long to take hold of the joy Jesus promises."

—**Alicia Bruxvoort**, writer,
speaker, abundant life seeker

Love Life Again

FINDING JOY WHEN
LIFE IS HARD

Tracie Miles

DAVID C COOK

transforming lives together

LOVE LIFE AGAIN
Published by David C Cook
4050 Lee Vance Drive
Colorado Springs, CO 80918 U.S.A.

Integrity Music Limited, a Division of David C Cook
Eastbourne, East Sussex BN23 6NT, England

The graphic circle C logo is a registered trademark of David C Cook.

LCCN 2018900965
ISBN 978-1-4347-1015-4
eISBN 978-0-7814-1445-6

The Team: Alice Crider, Margot Starbuck, Liz Heaney, Amy Konyndyk,
Rachael Stevenson, Kayla Fenstermaker, Susan Murdock
Cover Design: Nick Lee
Cover Photo: Getty Images

052718

*"I came so they can have real and eternal life,
more and better life than they ever dreamed of."*
John 10:10 (THE MESSAGE)

Contents

Acknowledgments

When God laid it on my heart to be a writer fifteen years ago, I remember thinking, *But Lord, I don't want to share "that." I'm afraid to be vulnerable and transparent. Can't I just share the good stuff?* Clearly, if you've ready any of my books, you know His answer to that question was no. He called me to be real, and He keeps giving me new experiences to do exactly that through my writing—not only to spread His love but also to help me continue to walk by faith and not sight.

I've often wished God hadn't called me to share so much of my life and all that goes on in the privacy of my heart and mind, but I've learned that doing so is not only a special calling but also a special gift from Him to enjoy. I've been blessed beyond belief at how God uses my realness and the words He alone gives me as the keys that will often open the door to someone else's heart so they can expose their own wounds to the only One who can heal them. That is the reason I write. But I couldn't do it alone.

To all the people at David C Cook. You have continued to believe in me, push me, and grant me grace so many times. I am so thankful.

To my editor, Margot Starbuck. You always help me be creative and think outside the box.

To my agent, Greg Johnson. You not only care about my writing opportunities but also about me as a person. Thank you for all your genuine concern, kind words, prayers, support, brainstorming phone calls, and patience with me as I sought God's leading and direction.

To my mom, Barbara. You have always been my biggest cheerleader and put up with me no matter what mood I am in. To say your love, support, generosity, and compassion have been overflowing the past few years as I've walked a hard road would be an understatement. Not everyone is blessed with a mother who is her friend, much less one who would do anything in the world, despite the sacrifice, for her child. But I am. I couldn't have made it this far without your unconditional love, never-ending positive outlook, and example of being the kind of person I long to be.

To my sister, Christie, and my brother, Tommy, and their families. Your support and love have been immeasurable. Even though you often didn't know what words to say or how to help, you have always been there for me, and I am grateful for you.

To my amazing children, Morgan, Kaitlyn, and Michael. You've watched me cry for hours while holding back your own tears. You've stood strong and helped me stand in my weakest moments, during times when I should have been standing strong for you instead. You've helped me always try to look at the positive side and keep trusting God, which helps me believe I must have done something right in raising you. You are amazing, incredible people. You've all three shown a maturity, wisdom, strength, and faith far beyond the years you have lived. I will never be able to thank God enough for giving me the privilege and blessing of being your mom, and I am honored to now have you as my best friends too. Having you to call my own is the thing I will forever be most proud of and the primary reason, besides God, that I can love my life every single day—no matter what. I am here for you, forever and always.

During difficult times, you find out who your true friends really are.

To my sisters at Proverbs 31 Ministries. Your support has been invaluable. Your ongoing prayers, acts of kindness, text messages, Facebook messages, private emails, and unwavering love and support has never been taken for granted and will never be forgotten. I love you all dearly.

To my closest friends from Pine Lake Country Club, who are my tennis buddies, slumber party roomies, wine connoisseurs, and fellow girls' trip lovers no matter the destination. I could not have survived the last few years without you. You have made me laugh, spent time with me, always included me, and loved me unconditionally. You've listened, let me lean on you, and even forgiven me when needed. You've stuck by me and supported me in every way you could. I don't know how I got so lucky, but you are all—every single one of you—an answer to prayer, and I attribute part of my healing and overcoming to the immense blessing of being your friend.

To my Jesus. Thank You for loving me enough to make me go through the hard stuff while helping me realize what it really means to fully depend on You and trust You for everything. You are faithful and good. You've never failed or abandoned me, and I know I am loved. I am grateful to be Your daughter.

Introduction

Before the plane even backed away from the gate, the captain gave us a disturbing warning: "It's been a rough day in the air, folks. Prepare yourself for tremendous turbulence."

As the words *tremendous turbulence* seeped into my mind, I wondered if it was too late to run for the door. I had a tight schedule, and our flight was already delayed, so I knew waiting for another flight wasn't an option. Plus, it was unlikely I'd be able to get off the plane, given that we had already backed away from the gate. So I tightened my seat belt, took a deep breath, and said a prayer for safety.

All was well the first thirty minutes of the flight, but then the captain's warning became a reality.

It was the worst turbulence I'd ever experienced. The plane rocked back and forth, up and down. Heads were bobbing, necks were jerking, and I could hear luggage sliding around in the overhead bins. When the flight attendant began distributing sickness bags, I wondered if I would soon need one.

To make matters worse, the pilot could not land the plane because of the high winds and heavy rain. After flying in circles around the airport for over an hour, the plane was running out of fuel. We couldn't wait any longer for the storm to blow past, so air traffic control rerouted our plane to another state, and we were finally able to land.

Yes, I said "another *state*," not another airport. And, yes, I said "running out of fuel."

I didn't really believe we would crash, but the possibility of that happening still made me a bit anxious. I knew plane crashes are typically avoidable and highly unlikely and our captain and flight crew were experienced and capable of getting us safely to our destination.

But still … *what if?*

What if the worst happened?

Was I ready to die? Had I lived life to the fullest? Did I have any regrets? Should I have done things differently? Should I have laughed more, loved stronger, hugged harder, and lived more abundantly? Should I have done more for other people? Had I let problems and busyness steal my ability to enjoy life?

That flight seemed to last forever and a day, and I had a lot of time to think. I thought about all my loved ones, especially my three precious children. What were my last words to them? Were they kind or harsh? Were they words filled with love or detailed instructions of what they were to do during my absence? When was the last time I had told my parents, siblings, and friends how much they meant to me?

Then my thoughts began heading in a new direction. Did I have any unfinished business, fences that needed mending, or people I needed to forgive and extend grace to? Were there friends I had been meaning to call or visit yet I hadn't taken the time to do so? Was there anything God had called me to do that I hadn't done because of lack of time, procrastination, or a fear of stepping out in faith? What had I done lately to serve others and be the hands and feet of Jesus?

My thoughts continued to spiral. If I never made it back home, had I prepared my children spiritually and emotionally to be able to handle life, follow their hearts, trust God, and walk in faith? Had I taught them life is precious and meant to be enjoyed? Did they know and believe it is possible to have a positive mind-set and live an optimistic, joy-filled life in good times and in bad? Had I been a good role model for living out these truths?

Had I lived as if I truly loved my life?

As I stared out my little oval window at the rain pelting the side of the plane, I intentionally began to fill my mind with new thoughts. All the things that had consumed my mind when I boarded the plane lost their urgency as I pondered the life I had been given and how I had been living it.

I began thanking God for all the gifts He had given me, starting with the small, everyday blessings I usually take for granted and ending with the people, things, pleasures, and faith that make my life worth living. I promised God and myself that if I ever got off that plane, I would intentionally and purposefully enjoy the life He had given me. I determined to be grounded in the truth, live the truth, and allow that truth to fill my mind with joy and contentment. To love my life every single day, even when problems or difficult circumstances raged around me, threatening to steal my joy.

I averted my gaze from the window and looked down at my travel bag, noticing my Bible sticking out of the top. I reached down and picked it up, determined to find a distraction from the storm outside and the one inside my head.

The first verse I looked at was James 4:14: "How do you know what your life will be like tomorrow? Your life is like the morning fog—it's here a little while, then it's gone." Wow! How timely, to say the least!

In this chapter, James was reprimanding the wealthy for making plans without acknowledging God's control over their lives and for their tendency to prioritize worldly things rather than things that were important from God's perspective. They had gotten so caught up in "doing life" and carrying out their oh-so-important plans that they had forgotten how priceless the gift of life truly was and overlooked the importance of making God the foundation of their thoughts, feelings, plans, and actions.

We too can get so caught up in our to-do lists, striving to achieve success, reach our goals, and acquire more stuff that we forget to love the life we've been given. Or we can become so consumed with focusing on all the things in our lives that aren't going as we would like and allow our adversities to rob us of joy and optimism and gradually develop a bitter, negative outlook. All of which causes us, much like the people James was addressing, to inadvertently take the gift of life for granted, neglect to aim for living with God's perspective, and forget all the reasons we have to be thankful for the life we've been given, even when it's not the life we thought we'd have.

Sweet friend, you don't have to search for a different life in order to enjoy life; you simply have to embrace the one you have by putting Christ at the center and asking Him to help you enjoy life, despite life.

In Ecclesiastes 3:12–13, Solomon summarized what he learned in his search for a happy life: "So I concluded there is nothing better than to be happy and enjoy ourselves as long as we can. And people should eat and drink and enjoy the fruits of their labor, for these are gifts from God." Simply put, Solomon realized we can't know how long we'll live on this earth. He discovered that life is a gift from God and is meant to be enjoyed.

When was the last time you felt joyful about your life? Regardless of what may be breaking your heart and stealing your ability to feel happy and joyful, God's desire is for you to delight in the life He is allowing you to live, starting today. In fact, He has already equipped you to enjoy life even during those seasons when you feel broken, confused, frustrated, overwhelmed, underappreciated, disillusioned, disappointed, or just plain bored with the humdrum of your life.

If you're longing to love life again, I invite you to join me on a journey to start doing exactly that. Within these pages you will find tips, tools, and practical steps to help you live life to the fullest. Everything you do as you learn to love your life again will be a faith-fueled step in the right direction. You can't change how you responded to yesterday, but you can change how you respond to tomorrow. It's within your power to experience the satisfying life you've been hoping for.

The first step to loving life again is believing it is possible for you.

Today can be the first day of the rest of your abundant, joy-filled life. Are you ready?

Embrace Contentment

There came a time I had to accept that my life had not turned out the way I thought it would and no amount of wishing it were different was going to change it.

I thought I had done all the right things and was on track for living out the life I envisioned. I graduated from college, got married, had three children, and pursued a career for fifteen years until deciding to be a stay-at-home mom. I had stayed committed to my promises and persevered through thick and thin. I had made my faith and following God a priority and even served in ministry. Although not perfect by any means, I had honored my marriage vows and tried my best to be a loving, devoted wife and the best mom I could be. I had kept my family and friends close. But sometimes on the road of life we come across an unexpected bump, causing our plans to get derailed and our hopes to be crushed. Then one day something tragic or life altering happens that drains the joy out of living, or we simply wake up and realize the life we are living is not the one we expected, much less the one we wanted.

Perhaps you can relate. Maybe you had a dream crushed after years of pursuing it. Perhaps you stayed at a job for thirty years, building your retirement fund, only to have that company go bankrupt and take your life savings down with it. Perhaps you've experienced the heartbreak of infertility when you planned on having a house full of children. Maybe you had a loved one die far too soon. Maybe you were struck with a disease that limits your abilities and independence. Maybe you thought you'd be married by now but are still single, or maybe you invested years in a marriage that ended in divorce.

I don't know what you've faced, but whatever happened that changed your life or rocked your world just may have snatched your love for life too. And as a result, maybe you don't think you can ever love life again.

Trust me, friend. I understand.

I had been married for twenty-six years, ten months, and five days when my divorce became final. After many painful months of separation, it had become obvious that reconciliation was not possible because of my husband's refusal to stop the behaviors and infidelity that caused the marriage to fail, leaving divorce as the only option. My heart was broken. My dreams of growing old with my husband—dancing arm in arm at our children's weddings, buying a beach house to enjoy together in retirement, celebrating future holidays and special occasions with our kids and their families, bouncing our grandbabies on our knees—were shattered the day he chose to leave the life we had built together.

As a woman, I felt rejected, betrayed, humiliated, devastated, afraid, and terribly alone.

As a mom, I felt overwhelmed with grief and worry about how this situation would permanently scar my children's hearts and helpless as to how ease their pain.

As the sole provider, I worried about having enough money to take care of my children's needs and keep us afloat. As weeks turned into months, bills were going unpaid, debt was piling up, and the home we'd lived in for over twenty years was in jeopardy of foreclosure. It seemed spiritual warfare was fierce, and bizarre things kept happening to me and my children. I perpetually felt overwhelmed and hopeless. Crippling fear, worry, and stress became my constant companions. The weight of all I was facing seemed almost too much to bear. I wondered if my heart would ever mend, if the hurt would ever lessen, if the loneliness would ever feel less lonely, and if I would ever feel strong, stable, and secure again.

I constantly grappled with the hardest question of all: *Would I ever be able to love life again?*

I spent every day consumed with despair and worry. I began to spend more time at home, depression sinking in, avoiding the emotional energy it would take to interact with people in public. I stopped doing many of the things I loved like playing tennis, shopping, and hanging out with friends. I took a sabbatical from doing ministry as my heart tried to heal. And I even stopped going to church to avoid the obligation of awkward small talk and a fake smile. Happiness and laughter seemed to be things of the past.

For the first time ever, I began keeping an extensive journal. I quickly realized it was a safe, private place for me to vent and pour out my feelings to God. Little did I know that this journal would become one of the things He would use to heal my heart and provide me with evidence of His work in my life.

On March 19, six months after my husband left, I wrote this entry:

> Spent an hour in prayer this morning after waking up crying … again. Feeling so overwhelmed with sadness and grief that I couldn't get a grip on my emotions. I just wish my life were different. It's not what I wanted it to be—for me or my children. I wish my family wasn't broken. I wish I could make everything better, but I just can't change or fix anything. I can't make my husband love me or want to be a part of our family. I can't heal my children's hearts. I can't ignore all the problems that cause me angst and worry. I'm tired. Tired of the stress and the emotional drain of this unfamiliar life. Tired of the heartache and pain. Tired of the fear. Tired of dealing with life. Physically, emotionally, and mentally tired. I try to put on a good face for the kids when they're home, although there are days when it's impossible to hold back the tears. And I try to be strong around others, but I feel like I'm losing who I am. I don't understand why all this has happened.
>
> "Lord, I don't want to be broken anymore. I want to be whole again. I want to feel whole and

complete, even if my marriage is over. Even though my heart is broken, I don't want to be a broken woman. I don't want to be a broken soul. I don't want to feel broken anymore. I want to enjoy life again. Fill me with joy, peace, and rest in You. I'm tired; give me strength. Restore to me the joy of my salvation. The ache in my soul is so deep; please lessen the ache. I don't understand why this has all happened and how it is all going to turn out. But I want to love my life again, right now, no matter what it looks like. Help me love life again, even while life is hard. Amen."

One day after writing that prayer, I read my daily devotional, and the truths I read reminded me not to let my desire to understand *why* I was going through this painful journey distract me from experiencing God's presence. It reminded me that God could indeed equip me to get through each day victoriously; I simply had to choose to let Him be the source of my joy, even in the midst of less-than-joyful circumstances of life.

Upon reading that devotional, I made the choice to stop letting my circumstances dictate my love for life. Over the many months that followed, I walked closely with God and implemented the steps I've outlined in this book. I have stumbled in my efforts more than once, but each time, I picked myself back up and started the next day afresh. I came to realize that it was not only within my reach to love my life again but also 100 percent within my control.

Friend, loving life is a choice, and we all have the power to choose to love our lives. Our own happiness is up to us. No person or circumstance has the power to take away our happiness or love for life without our permission. No matter what situation you find yourself in today, happiness is within your reach too.

If you're in a fragile, lonely, disheartened, or fearful place today—whatever that place looks like—please stick with me. I have learned it is possible to love our lives, despite what's going on or how much life has changed. My deepest prayer is that you will discover that it is possible for you to love your life again too.

But just maybe you're reading this and thinking that nothing big, dramatic, or life shattering has happened to derail your life or change it at all. In fact, life is the same as it has always been. Same ol' circumstances, different day. And therein lies the problem. You're bored and frustrated with life in general and often find yourself thinking, *Surely there has to be more to life than this.* It might seem as if everyone else's life is more exciting, more rewarding, easier, or simply better than yours. You feel let down by what life has given you or how it's turned out, and you're discontent. Maybe you even feel let down by God.

The truth is, regardless of what situation we find ourselves in, we all *want* to be excited about our lives. We know we *should* appreciate life even when it's hard and good is always present even during bad times, but it's a challenge to think that way when our hearts are heavy. We know we're *supposed* to be content, but we still get caught up striving for more or resenting what is not to our liking. And when life seems boring and routine, we often overlook the blessings God has given us because we're more focused on what we don't have than what we do.

It's challenging to be content in today's world. In fact, content-ment seems to have become a lost art. We are constantly bombarded with images of newer, bigger, and improved items that will suppos-edly make our lives happier, fuller, and more satisfying. We scroll through social media and feel discontent with our home, spouse, car, kids, vacations, clothes, shoes, and everything else because we think others have it better. We watch love stories on television and begin to feel unhappy with our own relationships as we compare them with those of fictional characters, or maybe even with real-life rela-tionships that seem better than our own. It's tempting to compare our lives with others' or think "If only …" but these thoughts open the door for discontentment, allowing it to sink into our hearts and minds and choke our joy. Discontentment sabotages our happiness.

Hebrews 13:5 says, "Don't be obsessed with getting more mate-rial things. Be relaxed with what you have" (THE MESSAGE). This verse instructs us not to look for happiness in money or material things. We are to be satisfied with the present and with what we have been given. To be content with where God has us in the present moment. Period.

FIGHT YOUR TRUE ENEMY

When life is hard or disappointing, it's easy to get stuck in a negative mind-set, especially when we feel as if life should be one way but instead it's another way entirely and we don't like it one bit. We feel stuck when it seems we've done everything possible to bring about change yet nothing seems to change at all. We feel stuck when we're constantly trying to manipulate things to go our way, control things that are out of our control, and change people who we have no power to change. When our lives are filled with obligations we "have to" meet or responsibilities we know we "should" or "must" do, we can feel as if we're caught in quicksand. We get stuck in discontentment, even if we have countless reasons to love our lives and feel thankful.

When I've felt stuck in a season I didn't want to be in, I've inadvertently lost sight of the fact that there was a war going on for my joy and happiness. I became so focused on the problems that I stopped focusing on the enemy I was really fighting.

John 10:10, the anchor verse for this book, reminds us, "The thief's purpose is to steal and kill and destroy." How often we forget this warning. All too often we think our enemy is society, people, circumstances, or hardships. But the reality is that Satan is our enemy, not people or circumstances. While he is not in control of this world and what happens, he can wage war on our hearts and minds. He can convince us that we have a right to be grumpy and no reason to be joyful. He can feed us nagging lies to keep us discouraged, angry, unforgiving, or without hope.

One of his most insidious lies is that God has it out for us. Satan loves to whisper this lie when bad things happen to us, things we don't deserve. But God is not the enemy. Satan is. God is always for us and never against us. Romans 8:31 says, "What shall we say about such wonderful things as these? If God is for us, who can ever be against us?" This verse doesn't promise we'll never experience persecution or pain, but it does affirm God is never against us. He is always fighting for us. Also, in 1 John 4:16 we read, "God is love." He is incapable of evil because love is the opposite of evil.

While it's Satan's goal to keep us stuck in discontentment, in John 10:10 we also see Jesus offer great hope that we don't have to live that way. He told His listeners,

> "My purpose is to give them a rich and satisfying life."

> "I came that they may have life and have it abundantly." (ESV)

> "I came so they can have real and eternal life, more and better life than they ever dreamed of." (THE MESSAGE)

Jesus died not just so we could have eternal life but so we could enjoy abundant life here on earth.

Does it excite you to think you can have a rich and satisfying life? An abundant life? A life better than you've ever dreamed of? A life you love? Me too! But maybe in the back of your mind, there is still that nagging voice telling you that happiness is not possible *for you* because _____ (fill in the blank with your why).

That, my friend, is the voice of the enemy. Don't listen to it. It is not coming from God, and is it not true.

To understand this promise of abundant life, it helps to look at the context of this verse. In John 10, Jesus taught that He is the shepherd and we are His sheep, and there is an enemy who seeks to steal, kill, and destroy us. But in verse 10, Jesus declared that He came to earth so we could not only live but live abundantly. He was conveying that He is the answer to experiencing the best life ever; He is what gives our lives meaning and joy.

William Barclay explained it this way:

> Jesus claims that he came that men might have life and might have it more abundantly. The Greek phrase used for *having it more abundantly* means to have *a superabundance of a thing*. To be a follower of Jesus, to know who he is and what he means, is to have a superabundance of life. A Roman soldier came to Julius Caesar with a request for permission to commit suicide. He was a wretched, dispirited creature with no vitality. Caesar looked at him. "Man," he said, "were you ever really alive?" When we try to live our own lives, life is a dull, dispirited thing. When we walk with Jesus, there comes a new vitality, a superabundance of life. It is only when we live with Christ that life becomes really worth living and we begin to live in the real sense of the word.[1]

You do not have to stay stuck in a life of unhappiness. You do not have to let your circumstances or other people dictate your ability to feel joy. You do not have to let discontentment poison your heart and mind and blind you to the wonderful life God has given you. The situations in your life may stay the same, but you do not have to live the same after today. You know who the enemy is; now stand up and fight.

WITHIN OUR REACH

Here's the thing: life is precious; our days are numbered. When we keep this in mind, it can motivate us to fight the enemy and live every day to the fullest.

According to Paul, we can learn to be happy with the life we have been given. In Philippians 4:12, he told the church at Philippi, "I have learned the secret of being content in any and every situation" (NIV). Considering the apostle Paul's difficult life, this is pretty amazing. He wrote these words while he was sitting in a dark, dirty prison cell. He had been arrested on false charges by corrupt officials and was facing the possibility of execution, yet he wrote he had learned to be content with whatever he had, which at the moment was literally nothing, not even his freedom. How could he feel that way after all he'd been through … and while he was in prison? Regardless of his circumstances and despite having endured much persecution and loss, Paul enjoyed peace and inner rest because his heart was right with God and he believed God was in control.

Contentment is a virtue we learn and develop through faith alone, and it plays a huge role in our happiness. When we are content, we are free to enjoy every blessing God has given us rather than constantly be searching for more. When we are content, we are resting in the knowledge that at the end of life, all that will really matter is our relationship with people we love, our relationship with God, and whether or not we lived life to the fullest. Nothing else is going to matter at all.

Let me be clear. God cares about what we want; He just doesn't want our wants to be more important to us than He is. Psalm 37:4 says, "Take delight in the LORD, and he will give you your heart's desires." In other words, when we put God first—above everything else—and want Him more than the stuff we wish we had or think we need, He will give us the desires of our hearts because those desires will align with what He wants for us. As Joyce Meyer once put it, "If we're lusting after something and we think we can't be happy without that, God's not going to give us that. Because then our joy is in the thing, not in Him."[2]

The life you are living today—and all it includes or doesn't include—is the life God has given you. It is the life you are supposed to love, despite what it might look like. It is the only life you have and the only life you are going to get. You can make the most of it and live it abundantly, or you can let life pass you by as you allow problems or drudgery to steal your zest for living. You can choose to be content and joyful, or you can choose to be disgruntled and sad.

The day I uttered that prayer of brokenness and heard God's voice after reading the devotional was the day I finally made this choice for myself. I was exhausted from waking up every day with an ache in my soul, wondering how I was going to make it through the day. I was tired of feeling stuck in unhappiness and in a difficult season and longed to feel inner joy and peace once again. One day after a deep time of prayer, I realized I could continue to wish things were different and obsess and cry over my problems, or I could determine to make things different inside my own heart and head. I could start fighting for my joy, or I could continue to let the enemy be in control of my happiness. I could courageously fight the war, or I could stay stuck and let the enemy win. In faith I boldly chose to deal with my unhappiness by embracing contentment.

You can make that choice too, starting today.

Life is not always a bed of roses. It's not always exciting. It's not always easy. It's not always fair. It's not always overflowing with opportunity and adventure. Consequently, we're all going to feel a sense of unhappiness or discontentment from time to time. We won't always feel like jumping out of bed in the morning and putting on our "I love my life!" T-shirts. But when we realize we are struggling with discontentment, that's the perfect time to choose to embrace contentment.

We can choose to embrace contentment when we struggle to make ends meet every month or can't afford that new outfit we really want. We can embrace contentment when we find ourselves secretly envying the relationships, marriages, or financial status of others. We can embrace contentment when our hearts are broken, when we lose people we treasured, or when life just seems to be giving us lemons.

Loving life is a choice, not a by-product of everything going our way. The choice to love life is ours, and our peace, joy, contentment, fulfillment, and overall happiness depend on the choice we make.

LOVE YOUR LIFE CHALLENGE #1

Recognize discontentment and reclaim authority over your happiness.

Reflect

Do you feel stuck in a negative season or mind-set that is stealing your joy?

How might your life change if you were to recognize and then address your discontentment by putting God first and choosing to fight for your happiness?

Act

Identify what change you believed needed to happen in order for you to be happy. Commit today to start choosing to be happy with the life you have, even if the desired change does not happen right away. Fully allow yourself to believe God hears your prayers and longs to meet the desires of your heart, but commit to living with joy and contentment as you wait to see God move in your circumstances, heart, and life.

Pray

Lord, I am committing to having a new take on life, starting today. I boldly reclaim my life and my joy from the enemy, who wants to steal, kill, and destroy it. I refuse to let him rob me of enjoying the life You have given me by poisoning my mind with discontentment. Today I choose to embrace contentment. In Jesus' name, amen.

Smile

Spend some time outside enjoying nature. Let the sunshine warm your skin. Listen for the sounds of birds or crickets. Take a deep breath and fill your lungs with fresh air. Take a leisurely walk, and rather than letting your mind park on problems, think about all the things that bring a smile to your face.

2

Recognize Your Value

Several years ago, I flopped down on my bed after a long, busy day and engaged in some mindless channel surfing. As usual, despite having hundreds of channels to watch, I couldn't find anything interesting. That is, until I came across a reality show so bizarre it caught my attention.

I'll confess I am not a fan of reality shows and typically don't watch any of them. I actually hate to admit I watched this one. But I did. I wasn't sure what the purpose of the show was, but when I realized what was happening, it broke my heart.

On this particular show, called *Dating in the Dark*, young men and women met for the first time—in pitch-black dark. They spent a couple of days together in a room—in pitch-black dark. They talked and asked questions about each other's backgrounds, interests, and personalities—in pitch-black dark.

After a few days of getting to know each other in the dark, the time would come for each couple to see each other in the light. The women on the episode I watched were beside themselves with anxiety, wondering how the men would react to how they looked. Would they like what they saw?

The deciding moment came. Each couple was brought into a still pitch-black room. Then a spotlight appeared on each person for a few seconds. It seemed to me in that moment what mattered most was each contestant's physical appearance. The three women on the show were beautiful. Not flawless, but still beautiful. My heart sank as I realized that their self-confidence could be lifted or shattered by the opinions and responses of the men they had been dating in the dark.

I was heartsick to hear what the men had to say when they got together. They mercilessly discussed each woman and how they were not what they expected. According to these men, the women were not as in shape as the women they normally dated. They were not as fashionable as they had hoped. They were not as pretty as the women they usually pursued. They were not as tall or short or voluptuous— or whatever. Simply put, these young women were less than perfect. They didn't measure up. They weren't enough. And all on national television. Gracious!

I cannot imagine the feelings of inadequacy these women must have experienced as they stood there, knowing they were being judged and wondering if they would pass the test, hoping someone would see their value. Their body language and eyes betrayed their nervousness, despite the smiles they had painted on for the camera. I am sure their minds were filled with anxious thoughts such as, *Will he still like me, now that he knows what I look like? Will he like what he sees? Am I pretty enough? Am I good enough? Am I thin enough? Am I smart enough? Will he approve of me? Will he want me?*

Unfortunately, none of the women on this particular episode received the feedback she longed for. Each one walked away, either in anger and defiance or pain and tears. I am confident these women also walked out questioning if they had value, not only to the handful of men on this reality show but to anyone at all. I'll bet that the critical words spoken about them echoed in their minds and when they looked in the mirror, they felt what they saw was no treasure.

I wish I could call each of these young women and tell her the criticism and judgment she received were not "reality." They were nothing more than biases founded on earthly standards and unrealistic expectations of perfection—by people who were themselves imperfect.

WE BELIEVE A LIE

Sadly, many, many women question whether they are lovable or worthy of love. Can you relate?

Maybe you weren't on a reality show where strangers criticized, humiliated, and rejected you, but you have people in your life who have done that—people who were supposed to care about you and protect you. It's one thing to be spurned by someone you hardly know; it's another to be rejected by those who know you well and are supposed to love and nurture you. Their critical words and hurtful treatment cut deep. They seep into your heart and burrow into your spirit, causing you to wonder if what those people have said about you really is true.

Or maybe you've made mistakes you wish you could undo.

Maybe someone abused you or violated you in some way.

Maybe you are struggling to break free of an addiction or a bad habit and just can't succeed, no matter how hard you try.

Please know that if you have questioned your value for any reason, you are not alone. You are not the only one who struggles to love the woman in the mirror.

Glamour magazine surveyed more than three hundred women of all sizes. They had to write down every negative thought they had about themselves. The results showed that the average woman has thirteen negative thoughts about herself and her appearance *every day*. That's close to one negative, self-condemning thought for every waking hour! Even more troubling was that a large number of women admitted to having thirty-five, fifty, or even one hundred negative thoughts about themselves every day, and 97 percent said they have at least one "I hate my body" moment per day.[1] This is the sad reality we live in.

Most of us struggle to accept and love ourselves, not only because of what we see in the mirror but also because of the sins, mess-ups, and imperfections we are keenly aware of but no one else can see. Satan uses every tactic possible to keep our confidence and self-esteem in the dirt, including the thoughts in our heads. Although he can't hear our thoughts because he's not omniscient, he can hear our negative self-talk if spoken aloud. And he can use the words or treatment of others to impact how we think about ourselves if we allow the lies to become truths in our minds.

Regardless of the reason you don't feel valuable or worthy, it is a flat-out lie. God's Word says otherwise, and His Word is true. End of story. If only we believed in our core that we have great value in God's eyes! If you are like many women I know, you know this truth from Scripture, but that doesn't keep you from letting the criticism of others or the lies in your own head cause you to question your worth.

Why do we constantly compare ourselves with others and tear ourselves down as inferior when we know that leads only to disappointment and lowered self-esteem?

Why do we allow criticism to creep into the deepest, most sensitive parts of our hearts, instead of remembering we are beautiful because of *Whose* we are, not because of what we see in the mirror?

Why?

Because we are human. Because we feel week or beaten down by life or others. Because we know we are imperfect. Because we are fully aware of every one of our shortcomings and flaws. Because we live in a broken world. And because the enemy of our souls wants us to continue feeling unlovable, unacceptable, and unworthy. He wants us to see ourselves negatively and forget how valuable we are to Christ because he knows when we hold on to those negative misconceptions, we're less likely to live with joy and happiness, and won't fully embrace the joy and freedom available in Christ.

Ephesians 6:12 says, "For we are not fighting against flesh-and-blood enemies, but against evil rulers and authorities of the unseen world, against mighty powers in this dark world, and against evil spirits in the heavenly places." Emphasis here on *dark*. The enemy, who lurks in the dark, would love to tear down our self-esteem. He

knows if he can weaken our confidence through lies, self-condemnation, and the hurtful words of others, our faith may become weak as
well, and we certainly won't love who God created us to be or the life
He has given us.

In the dark and behind the scenes, Satan works against us, hoping we will succumb to insecurities and doubt and deny our value in
Christ. He wants us to feel "less than" so we will live a "less than" life
and not experience—or even seek—the abundant life promised to
the treasured possessions of Jesus Christ. He wants us to believe we
have to be perfect to be priceless.

But God says otherwise.

HERE'S THE TRUTH: YOU ARE A TREASURE

Jesus declares you are one of His greatest treasures, precious in His
sight. "Others were given in exchange for you. I traded their lives for
yours because you are precious to me. You are honored, and I love
you" (Isa. 43:4). "For you are a chosen people. You are royal priests,
a holy nation, God's very own possession. As a result, you can show
others the goodness of God, for he called you out of the darkness
into his wonderful light" (1 Pet. 2:9).

We are God's chosen ones. His beloved. His royal daughters. His
girls. We were important enough for Jesus to be crucified for sins we
hadn't even committed yet, because He saw us as valuable. Treasures
worth keeping forever in heaven.

Deuteronomy 26:18 says, "And the LORD has declared this day that you are his people, his treasured possession as he promised" (NIV). In Hebrew the word for "possession" describes the treasure of kings. Kings and leaders protect and value their treasured possessions.

In Deuteronomy 7:6, we read that *we* are a treasure. "For you are a holy people, who belong to the LORD your God. Of all the people on earth, the LORD your God has chosen you to be his own special treasure." In this passage the Lord was telling Israel they were His most valued possession—something He treasured because He was convinced of their worth. You see, He handpicked Israel, viewing them as more priceless than all the jewels known to humankind.

Friend, we are now God's Israel! You. Me. God loves every one of us. He holds us dear. We each have value in His eyes, not because of anything we have done or because of how others view us or because of what we look like. God values us because we are His. Because of who He is. The God who created us. The God who loves. The God who is love.

God chose the people of Israel and loved them, despite their history of idolatry, unbelief, and betrayal. Deuteronomy 7:7–8 says, "The LORD did not set his heart on you and choose you because you were more numerous than other nations, for you were the smallest of all nations! Rather, it was simply that the LORD loves you."

The same is true for why He chose you and me. It wasn't because we are perfect, because other people think we're valuable, or because we're the prettiest, thinnest, smartest, most talented, and most faultless people who ever were. He chose us simply because He loves us.

Just for a moment, let your mind wander to how life might be if you stopped criticizing yourself for everything you are not and instead started giving yourself credit for everything God says you are. If you started believing your value comes from God and nothing anybody says or does takes away from that value.

How much more could you enjoy life if you were happy with whom God created you to be? Have you ever considered how your disdain for or criticism of yourself is standing in the way of your ability to love your life? I promise you, there is a huge connection. Even though your thoughts are inside your head, if those thoughts are negative and self-defeating, they can wreck your life and steal your joy for living.

But even when we know the truth in our heads, it can be difficult to get our hearts in line. In fact, the idea that you have value and are worthy of love might seem irrational after all the years you've been beating yourself up, all the ways you know you've failed, all the hurtful words or actions of others, and all the flaws you see in the mirror every day.

I understand. I spent far too many years not loving the woman staring back at me in the mirror. No matter how good a Christian I tried to be, I would always stumble in one way or another, and the enemy would whisper reminders of my sins and mistakes, weakening my already fragile self-esteem and confidence. No matter how great a mom, devoted a wife, or faithful a friend I tried to be or how successful I was in my career, there was always this little voice in the back of my head telling me I wasn't good enough. It took many years of walking closely with God for me to truly understand the depth of His love for me; accept who I was, imperfections and all; and start seeing myself as His treasured, beloved possession.

KEEPING SELF-CONDEMNING THOUGHTS AT BAY

Despite having learned years earlier to believe in my value in Christ, it became harder than ever for me to see myself as a treasure after my marriage ended. In fact, every day the enemy's lie of "You were never enough" echoed through my mind again and again. I felt discarded. Disposable. Neither of which are words used to describe a treasure. Gradually my negative thoughts began to take a toll not only on my confidence and self-esteem but also on my joy. Fortunately, I was well aware of the impact of our thoughts on our lives as a result of writing my last book, *Unsinkable Faith*, so I knew I needed to get my thoughts under control so they could no longer control me or my happiness.

I bowed my head, closed my eyes, and asked God to give me an acute awareness of my thoughts so that each time I started condemning myself, believing something that was not true according to God's Word, I could recognize the lie, reject it, and replace it with something true about myself instead. Day after day I continued this practice, intently focusing on changing the way I thought about myself and my life. I learned to stop my critical thoughts in their tracks and change the words I was saying to myself. I forced myself to rehearse, "If you don't have anything good to say, don't say anything at all." While this is often said in reference to what we say about others, it can also be applied to what we say about ourselves. We should refuse to believe and say things about ourselves that are critical and mean, especially if they are things we would never say to someone else. We should always be as kind to ourselves as we would be to others.

Some days I even spoke out loud when I started thinking hopeless and critical thoughts about myself and my future. For example, I might tell myself, "Tracie, what you just said is not true, and you know it. And God would never say that about you, because you are valued in His eyes. So don't you say it to yourself either!"

I know, I know. That sounds a bit crazy. But I'm telling you, continually practicing taking control over my own thoughts helped me to be conscious of what I was telling myself and how I was damaging my own self-confidence. It also helped me see how it must break God's heart when I talk about myself, His daughter, in such hurtful ways. It opened my eyes to see how often I was focusing on thoughts that were untrue. Thoughts that were robbing me of my joy and squelching my zest for believing an abundant life was still possible for me.

Over time this small habit equipped me to embrace God's truths again and believe them with without doubt. Precious truths that I was enough and always would be and I was a treasure to Him. In fact, just maybe I was a treasure to a lot of people. Which I now believe I am—and so are you.

Lindsay also struggled for many years with thinking poorly of herself. Although she still isn't perfect at keeping her self-condemning thoughts at bay, she is more aware of those thoughts when they creep up and is better at rejecting them before they poison her mind. She said, "I try to stop myself in the middle of the thought and say, 'Get thee behind me, Satan.' Then I pray to ask God for help in the attack and strength to correct these thoughts and fight these battles."

I love that Lindsay recognized her negative self-talk was from the enemy and she was under a spiritual attack. It truly is a battle to see ourselves as God sees us! My friend Cheryl calls these thoughts "fiery darts of the evil one" (Eph. 6:16 ASV) and said she also rebukes them in Jesus' name. But she admitted that even still, they often come back and she has to continually remind herself to replace them with God's truths instead.

Jesus sees us through the lens of love and grace, but we often see ourselves through the lens of criticism, the scars of rejection, or the regrets of past mistakes. We think our thoughts don't matter, especially when they are about ourselves and not others. Yet the damage they can do has immeasurable impact on our confidence, relationships, and overall outlook on life.

Kristy also found herself fighting the battle for her thoughts. She has sticky notes on most of the mirrors in her house, reminding her of who God says she is. She said, "The Scriptures are wonderful reminders and have helped me change my stinkin' thinkin' about myself." We need to do whatever it takes to fight the battle for our thoughts and start believing we are treasures in God's eyes.

We can't love our lives if we don't first love ourselves.

THIS IS THE DAY

Sweet friend, today is a brand-new day. A day to stand proud.

A day to start seeing yourself through God's eyes and not through your own tainted perspective or someone else's.

A day to celebrate that you are His special treasure.

A day to once and for all look in the mirror and see yourself as a unique jewel, precious and full of luster and beauty in every way because God uniquely created you and broke the mold—on purpose.

A day to remember you are adored and God loves you more than you could ever put into words. He loves you in the dark and in the light, no matter what, because you are His treasured possession. Moving from negative talk to truth talk will not only change how you think about yourself, it will also change your entire life.

Today is the day to start loving life again and seeing yourself through the lens of God's Word. Give some thought to what you can do to overcome the pull toward self-condemnation. Victory isn't going to happen just because you want it too. Every battle takes effort, and the battlefield in our minds is worth the fight.

Think about how you can begin refuting the enemy's lie that you are not valuable. What can you do every day to stand in confidence about who God made you to be? What works for one person may not work for another, so consider what weapon you want to use to fight. Maybe you can search for Scriptures that confirm your value in Christ. Memorize those verses or write them on sticky notes and put them on every mirror in your house like Kristy did.

If it takes displaying them on your refrigerator, car dashboard, and computer screen, then do that too! Over time God's Word in our hearts can override the words of the enemy.

Maybe it will help if you rebuke Satan out loud every time a self-critical thought starts worming its way into your mind. If you're in a public place when it happens, rebuke that thought mentally instead. Or keep a little spiral notebook or journal in your purse. Each time a condemning thought enters your mind, write it down, then scratch it out, confirming that the thought has no validity. Then write down what God says about you. After a while, you will be able to clearly see what thoughts you struggle with the most. Be sure to surrender those thoughts in prayer every day and seek God's help in replacing them with thoughts that build up His daughter, not tear her down.

Today is the day to begin taking steps to recognize your value. Learning to see ourselves the way God does is not always easy, but it is always possible. It takes time, but it will happen when we allow God's words about us to replace our own. When we learn to truly recognize our value as His treasured possessions, we swing open the door to loving life again.

LOVE YOUR LIFE CHALLENGE #2

Believe you are a treasure to God.

Reflect

Do you let the critical words or opinions of others steal your confidence and determine your value and sense of worth?

How does the constant struggle of trying to measure up to the expectations of others steal your love for living?

Act

Get out two pieces of paper. On one, jot down the critical words others have said to you and the critical words you say to yourself (all the lies you believe about yourself that contradict God's Word). On the other piece, write down all the good things about yourself you love and other people love about you—your gifts, talents, skills, smile, personality, sense of style, work ethic, etc. Which of these pieces of paper would make God smile? Which would bring a tear to His eye? The list of negative, critical words is not from Him. Tear it into tiny pieces and throw it away. Then tape the other one to your bathroom mirror. Read this list every day and add to it as you think of other things that make you special.

Pray

Father, I am so grateful for the truth of Your Word about who I am in You. Please help me see myself as You do. Help me see myself as the treasure You say I am and to live each day with a confidence that comes from You, not from my efforts, appearance, or accomplishments, much less the words, actions, or opinions of others. In Jesus' name, amen.

Smile

Break out of the norm and go on an adventure in your own city. Check out a new restaurant, tourist attraction, bubbling brook, or beautiful garden. Take pictures of things that make you smile, and think about how God is smiling down at you.

3

Love Yourself

I was driving on the interstate one beautiful sunny day. The windows were down, and the wind was blowing my hair in every direction, but I didn't care. The radio was blaring one of my favorite worship songs, and I was singing along at the top of my lungs.

All of a sudden I realized I was feeling something I hadn't felt in a long time: freedom and happiness. Freedom from self-condemnation. Happiness with who God had made me to be. Freedom from the pain, sadness, and fear that had been holding me hostage since my divorce. Freedom to embrace joy and peace in the life I was living. I realized that even though my circumstances and problems had not changed, I had. I felt free to be me and free to be happy.

I stopped singing and thanked God for all He had been doing in my life over many painful months of suffering. (I'll share more about God's intervention, protection, and provision in the following chapters.) Throughout this difficult journey, I had a clear sense of His presence. God had never left me, although it had been a hard-fought battle in my mind to get to that place of freedom. I believe He had been waiting for me to see myself again the way He saw me—perfectly created and loved by Him. Perfectly equipped to live abundantly in the season of life I was in, despite what that season looked like.

I thanked Him for all the blessings I enjoyed every day, even down to the gift of hearing music on the radio. I intentionally started thinking about good things, not just about my life but also about myself. Things like the gifts, talents, and skills God has blessed me with. The hobbies I enjoy like playing tennis, reading, dancing, and even just sitting on my deck listening to music. The fun and intriguing things I am interested in. The places I like to visit and the sports events I love going to with friends and family. My love for the beach and the water and all my fond memories there.

Rather than obsessing over who I wasn't, which is what I had been doing for years, I began to ponder who I really was. I had felt unimportant and like I didn't measure up for so long that it took awhile to rediscover my value and start liking and accepting who God had created me to be.

My circumstances were still the same. My heart was still sad over the breakup of my marriage, and I was still living in the wake of destruction it had caused. There were still plenty of legal and financial issues and worries to manage. I was still heartbroken for my children. I was still an imperfect person in need of the grace of a Savior. But I finally understood I had the capacity to love my life and myself, solely because I was loved by God. I simply had to choose to do so.

You see, before I could truly love my life, I realized I needed to learn to love myself again first.

CHERISH WHO YOU ARE

All too often we forget to truly cherish who we each are—a person God uniquely knit together in our mother's womb. We often find it easy to shower other people with love, overlook their flaws, and forgive them when needed, but we refuse to consider showing ourselves that same type of unconditional love. I know it sounds somewhat self-centered to say "Love yourself," or even "Cherish yourself," but Jesus Himself commands us to do so.

In Mark 12, we read of Jesus being tested by the religious leaders of Israel, who were completely opposed to His teachings, particularly His claims to be the Messiah. They were doing everything possible to catch Him in a lie or push Him to say something that would justify His arrest. They wanted to find fault with Him and put an end to His ministry, but no matter what they did, He rose above it.

> One of the teachers of religious law was standing there listening to the debate. He realized that Jesus had answered well, so he asked, "Of all the commandments, which is the most important?"
>
> Jesus replied, "The most important commandment is this: 'Listen, O Israel! The LORD our God is the one and only LORD. And you must love

> the LORD your God with all your heart, all your
> soul, all your mind, and all your strength.' The
> second is equally important: 'Love your neighbor
> as yourself.' No other commandment is greater
> than these." (vv. 28–31)

In this passage, Jesus was reiterating the truth told in Deuteronomy 6:5: "And you must love the LORD your God with all your heart, all your soul, and all your strength." Jesus followed up His command to love the Lord with all our hearts by saying it is equally important for us to love others as we love ourselves. Many of us overlook the last part of the second commandment. We focus on loving Jesus and others but discount the importance of loving ourselves.

But how can we love other people if we don't love ourselves first? We cannot demonstrate on the outside what we don't have on the inside, which is why we have to be nice to ourselves first and foremost. As we learn to embrace who we are and the way God made us, we become better equipped for loving our lives. When we have confidence in who we are and in Whose we are and feel good about ourselves, we are more likely to feel good about our lives overall. Self-confidence empowers us to be more optimistic, positive, and hopeful.

You and I might not be where we need or want to be on the self-confidence scale just yet, and we will always have room for improvement. However, we are still called to embrace who we are as children of God and His unconditional forgiveness, accept our imperfections and weaknesses, and be aware of all the unique and wonderful things about ourselves that God divinely designed. When we love God and ourselves, we can better love others.

To love yourself is to appreciate who God made you to be and who you really are. Not what your past says you are, not what other people say you are, and not what you say to yourself. To love yourself is to accept yourself.

BELIEVING WE ARE FEARFULLY AND WONDERFULLY MADE

The other day I was getting ready for church and my daughter Kaitlyn and I were in the bathroom brushing our hair and putting on makeup; doing what girls do. I apparently made several critical comments about myself: what a bad hair day I was having, how I had too many wrinkles, and how I needed to lose a few pounds. Kaitlyn looked me in the eye and said, "Mom, you cannot leave this room until you say three nice things about yourself." I laughed. But she was serious and kept insisting I not leave the bathroom until I had met her request. I finally gave in and said three nice things about myself. She moved away from the door and said, "Okay, you're free to go." Gee, thanks, honey. Can we say "role reversal"?

We laughed about our little conversation, but this story just proves how quickly and easily we fall into the habit of putting ourselves down, not only with our thoughts but also with our mouths. We may not even realize we are doing it until someone points it out.

It's funny how what we teach our kids when they're little comes full circle at times, which is what happened when Kaitlyn forced me to say three nice things about myself. You see, I had spent years trying to teach her and my other children how God sees them, that they are valuable in His eyes, and her words to me proved she understood what I'd been trying to instill in her.

I thought back to a time in Kaitlyn's life when she was struggling to love and accept herself. She was in the sixth grade and at that awkward stage in a young girl's life where loving what you see in the mirror is a hard-fought task. Despite that, Kaitlyn had begged for months to participate in a local beauty pageant. I was against it for many reasons but finally surrendered to her pleas, although letting her know we couldn't afford to spend several hundred dollars on a fancy new pageant gown. She said she was perfectly okay with that since she already had a beautiful tea-length gown we had purchased recently for another formal occasion.

After months of anticipation and preparation, the day of the pageant finally came, and Kaitlyn looked stunning. Her bright royal-blue, sequin-covered, tea-length dress made her blue eyes sparkle more brightly than usual. Her hair fell in long blonde locks across her shoulders. Lip gloss and glittery blue eye shadow made her look more grown up than she really was. She was beaming with confidence and joy as I dropped her off at the front door of the auditorium so she could hurry inside. But twenty minutes later, it was an entirely different scenario.

Our family was seated among all the other families when we noticed Kaitlyn's little face peeking through the big blue velvet curtains, her eyes scouring the auditorium for our whereabouts. Upon spotting us, she emerged from behind the curtain and made a beeline to our location. As she approached us, I could see big tears in her eyes. I asked her what was wrong, wondering what could have possibly happened to destroy the confident demeanor she had portrayed just moments earlier. She looked down at the floor and said, "Mommy, all the girls are wearing full-length gowns, and I am only wearing a short, tea-length gown. And I look so ugly and horrible. I will never win. I shouldn't have even signed up for this."

My heart broke. To my little girl, all that mattered was what was on the outside—how she measured up to the appearance and presumed standards of those around her, not what was on the inside. In her mind, not only did her dress fall short, but she did too.

I spent the next few minutes wiping away her tears and reassuring her of how beautiful she was, inside and out. I hugged her tight and explained that win or lose, she was beautiful because of who she was not what she was wearing. I told her how precious she was because she loved Jesus and because of the sweet compassion and kindness tucked in her little heart for everyone and everything.

Kaitlyn was able to regain her composure and later strutted onto the stage with poise and confidence. I was beaming with pride to be her mommy. Although she didn't win the pageant that day, she walked away with a much greater reward than a fake crown and a gold trophy fashioned out of plastic. She embraced God's truth about who she was and how much she was adored by Him and her family, and that was all that mattered.

As I think back to this memorable teaching experience with my daughter and my own lifelong struggles with loving and accepting myself, Psalm 139:14 comes to mind: "I praise you because I am fearfully and wonderfully made; your works are wonderful, I know that full well" (NIV). God reassures us through His Word that we are precious and beautiful, but all too often we do not know it *full well*, much less believe it *full well*. He wants us not only to *know* about being His wonderful creations—priceless treasures—but to *believe* it with every ounce of our being. He wants us to believe it when our view of ourselves is skewed because we are caught in the trap of comparison. To believe it when we feel as if we can't measure up to the perceived perfections of everyone around us. To believe it when hurtful words or actions threaten to make us feel inferior or inadequate.

Let's face it. Forgetting we are beautiful in God's eyes—the only eyes that matter—is not just a little-girl problem; it's a big-girl problem too.

Dove has been focusing on helping women increase their self-esteem for several years through a series of advertising campaigns. They conducted a study on the self-esteem of women. Below are some of the disheartening results:

- "Only 4% of women around the world consider themselves beautiful....

- 72% of girls feel tremendous pressure to be beautiful

- 80% of women agree that every woman has something about her that is beautiful, but do not see their own beauty

- More than half of women globally (54%) agree that when it comes to how they look, they are their own worst beauty critic."[1]

Every day we are faced with opportunities to compare ourselves with people we work with or go to school with. With people in our neighborhoods and communities, in magazines and television shows, and even in our churches and other ministries. We scroll through Facebook and Instagram and tell ourselves everyone is prettier, happier, more successful, better dressed, and much more perfect than we are. We think other women's marriages are so much better than ours, their husbands are more loving than ours, and their kids are more perfect than ours. We assume everyone we know is probably kinder, less self-centered, more talented, and more capable than we are—and we are less-than in more ways than one.

Such thoughts make loving ourselves impossible.

This faulty line of thinking keeps us from recognizing we are whole, complete, beautiful, accepted children of God, made in His image (see Gen. 1:27). It causes us to forget that He formed us in the womb (see Jer. 1:5). He created us beautifully and uniquely, exactly as we were supposed to be in every way. Gifted. Usable. Precious. Beautiful.

None of us is perfect, but every one of us is fearfully and wonderfully made, created on purpose with purpose. No wonder the second most important commandment highlights the importance of loving ourselves!

An important part of loving ourselves is taking care of ourselves. Let's take a look at what that means.

TAKE CARE OF YOURSELF

We have a hundred items on our to-do lists, all of which are urgent, and none of those items involves caring for ourselves. We have kids, husbands, friends, extended family, and bosses who all have priorities for us, so we put our own wants and desires at the bottom of every list. We're so busy meeting everyone else's needs we often forget about our own.

God designed women to be nurturers and doers. He formed us with instincts to love others, care about the needs of others, and put others before ourselves. This is good because it makes it easier for us to obey God's command to love others. But when we put ourselves so far down on the list of priorities that we never take time for self-care, we suffer emotionally, mentally, and physically. We are much more equipped to love and serve others when we take care of our own needs first.

I can't help but think about the safety instructions given at the beginning of every flight—instructions I definitely paid attention to on that unforgettable flight I talked about in the introduction of this book. They sound something like this: "In the event of a change in cabin air pressure, an oxygen mask will automatically drop down in front of you. To start the flow of oxygen, pull the mask toward you and place it firmly over your nose and mouth, securing the elastic band behind your head. Then breathe normally. If you are traveling with a child or someone who requires assistance, secure your own oxygen mask first and then assist the other person." Airline companies know that if you don't take care of yourself first, you will not be able to help others. What's true in the air is true on the ground as well.

As believers, we are to "seek first the kingdom of God" (Matt. 6:33 ESV). Until we put God first in our lives, nothing will feel right. But after that, we need to take care of ourselves. Jesus serves as our role model for doing exactly that. There were times He knew He needed to get away and focus on His relationship with the Father so He could fulfill the purposes His Father had equipped Him for. Jesus recognized His own needs and then took time to meet them. He knew if He was emotionally empty and physically exhausted, He could not minister to others.

Here are a few examples of times Jesus stepped away from ministry in order to do some self-care.

- In Luke 6:12, Jesus prayed all night on a mountain. He knew stressful times were on the horizon and He needed to take time for Himself and His soul.

- After the loaves and fishes incident, when Jesus fed more than five thousand men, women, and children, He sent the crowd home and then "went up into the hills by himself to pray" (Matt. 14:23). He needed time to rest and be refreshed—physically, mentally, and spiritually—so He would be ready to serve others again.

- After a busy day of preaching to crowds of people, Jesus and the disciples climbed into a boat to get away. He needed to rest, to be refueled physically, before He could continue meeting the needs of others, so He stopped to rest and take care of Himself when He felt the need to do so (see Mark 4).

In the three years of His ministry, Jesus cared for and met the needs of countless others. He preached and taught unceasingly. He fed thousands, raised the dead, and healed the sick. He was the Son of God, but He was also human. He too experienced physical and emotional exhaustion. But He didn't push aside His own needs and tend only to others; He took time to care for Himself too. If Jesus took time for self-care, shouldn't we? Why do we think we don't need and deserve that as well? If He made it a priority, we should too.

If we work, serve, and give tirelessly to others but never take care of ourselves or allow our needs to occasionally take precedence, it affects our ability to live life to the fullest and be whom God called us to be—and we might reach our breaking point. How can we love life if we are exhausted, burned out, and depleted?

Friend, if you want to find joy again, love yourself enough to take care of yourself—and don't feel guilty for doing so! Find ways to nurture yourself spiritually, physically, socially, emotionally, and intellectually. Think about what refreshes your heart, spirit, soul, mind, and body. Maybe it's taking a bubble bath, spending a night out with friends, reading a good book, or a taking a scenic drive. Maybe what restores your spirit is a day on the beach, a weekend getaway, a date night with your spouse, or quality time with family. Maybe for you self-care means eating things that are healthy and exercising regularly so you can feel better physically and have more energy.

Starting today, make loving yourself a priority in your life. Pay attention to when you need rest and restoration, and take time for some self-care. You are a priority in God's eyes, so start seeing yourself and treating yourself like a priority as well. It's so much easier to love our lives when we feel good, which happens when we love and take care of ourselves.

LOVE YOUR LIFE CHALLENGE #3

Commit to loving whom God created you to be.

Reflect

Do you love and accept yourself the way God wants you to? What change can you make today to start loving whom God created you to be?

Have you been so consumed with taking care of the needs of others that you have forgotten to take care of yourself? How do you think this impacts your peace and joy on a daily basis?

Act

Jot down a few ideas for how you can begin taking care of your spiritual, physical, mental, and emotional needs today. Be specific and allow yourself to dream big about what you'd like to focus on and the changes you'd like to implement that will benefit you as a person. Set some specific goals for implementing these new habits in your daily life and keep track over time of how you're doing. If life starts getting in the way, ask God to help you refocus and stay committed to your goals.

Pray

Dear Jesus, I want to love myself and believe I am a treasure and an amazing woman, just as You created me to be. Help me to stop looking at my flaws, imperfections, and struggles and start seeing myself through the lens of Your Word. Help me forget the words or actions of others that feed critical lies into my mind and to keep Your words about me at the forefront of my thoughts. In Your name, amen.

Smile

Do something to treat yourself today. Buy a new outfit, get a fresh hairstyle, visit your favorite coffee shop, exercise, or cook your favorite meal. Think about what will restore and refresh your heart, soul, body, and mind. Then do it!

4

Accept Forgiveness

It was just one little quote, but it stirred up a lot of feelings. In *Anxious for Nothing*, Max Lucado wrote, "There is a guilt that sits in the soul like a concrete block and causes a person to feel bad for being alive. There is a guilt that says, *I did bad*. And then there is a guilt that concludes, *I am bad*."[1] All my life I have known and believed God loves me. After all, the Bible tells me so. But because of one mistake I made as a young woman, I felt that I not only *did* bad but *was* bad. Shame and guilt consumed my heart and mind.

You see, at the age of nineteen with one year of college under my belt, I got pregnant and decided to have an abortion. I had no idea my heart would be forever scarred or that my decision would haunt me for decades. Although I continually asked for God's forgiveness and was indeed forgiven, I didn't believe in my heart He actually had forgiven me. Why? Because I didn't believe I deserved it. Actually, I knew I didn't deserve it.

Consequently, I wasted many years refusing to believe God loved me enough to forgive me for my sins, much less forget about them, which is one thing that fed into my constant lack of self-esteem. My doubts about His unconditional love and His promise to forgive and remember my sin no more (see Heb. 8:12) often cast a shadow on my faith. I had a mental picture of what He looked like when I kept asking for forgiveness for one mistake over and over, as well as for new sins I had committed. I envisioned Him sitting on His heavenly throne, looking down on me with a solemn look on His holy face. With His head resting in His hands, He would sigh and say, "*Tsk, tsk, tsk.* Poor child, she just can't get her act together. What is wrong with her? How many times do I need to forgive her? How many times is she going to ask? Gracious."

But when I was in my midthirties, everything changed. God touched my heart during a powerful worship service and lit a fire in my spirit to believe He is who He says He is; to start believing wholeheartedly that all His promises are true, including His promise of forgiveness; and to live passionately for Him. As if the scales of deception fell from my eyes, I could finally see and believe that I too was God's precious and beloved child, worthy of being forgiven and cleansed from my sins, both past and present.

Nothing is beyond God's compassion or ability to forgive. *Nothing.* Whether we deserve forgiveness is not a question God ponders, because He already sent His Son to take care of that. When we ask to be forgiven, we are.

ACCEPT GOD'S FORGIVENESS

The guilt and shame I had carried for years was not from God. He had not been beating me up over my mistakes for years. I had done that to myself. He had forgiven and forgotten my sin the very first time I asked for forgiveness, just as we're assured in Isaiah 43:25: "I—yes, I alone—will blot out your sins for my own sake and will never think of them again." I finally allowed myself to believe that 1 John 1:9 wasn't just meant for everyone else but was also meant for me: "If we confess our sins, he is faithful and just and will forgive us our sins and purify us from all unrighteousness" (NIV).

Jesus died for *every* sinner not just some, including you and me. Peter confirmed this in Acts 10:34 when he said, "I see very clearly that God shows no favoritism." He had learned through faith that Jesus will accept and forgive anyone who professes belief in Him. There is peace for all people through the Lord. God does not pick and choose who or what to forgive; He forgives us for anything when we ask Him.

I'll never forget how my heart leaped with joy and peace entered my spirit the moment I embraced God's gift of unconditional love, grace, and forgiveness for my mistake. I only wished I had accepted it years earlier, rather than listening to the lies of the enemy and giving him instead of God dominion over my happiness. Once I accepted God's grace and forgiveness, my soul came back to life and my heart was restored. I changed. All for the better.

My friend, do you believe God can forgive everything you have ever done? If you and I were sitting together on a park bench, talking and people-watching and enjoying the warm sunshine, what would you say if I asked you whether you believe Jesus can and will forgive you of your sins and toss them into the deepest sea, never to be thought of again?

If your answer would be yes—you believe He has forgiven all your sins—then fabulous! But if your answer would be no or you are unsure, this could be the stumbling block keeping you from loving yourself and your life. Will you pray right now and ask God not only to forgive you for your sins but also to help you embrace that forgiveness for the amazing free gift it is? Will you pray for Him to help you be free of the memories that haunt you and to help you let go of shame, guilt, and regrets so you can be filled with His peace and joy instead?

Peace and joy cannot reside where shame, regret, and guilt are living. Fortunately, we get to choose which of these feelings live in our hearts. While we may not be able to forget all our sins, we can ask God for the power to stop thinking about and obsessing over them. Philippians 4:8 says, "Fix your thoughts on what is true, and honorable, and right, and pure, and lovely, and admirable. Think about things that are excellent and worthy of praise." When we ask for and receive forgiveness, our slate is wiped clean. God declares us not guilty. Shame-ridden thoughts about our mistakes are not lovely or admirable. They are not excellent and worthy of praise. So rather than think about your regrets and wrongdoings, fill your mind with the beautiful truth that God has lavished you with grace and forgiveness. Let the past go, my friend.

It took me a while to let go of the past and believe God had forgiven me for what I had done. But when I did, I was able to start loving myself and embracing God's love for me. Accepting His forgiveness not only changed my heart but also my life overall. I no longer questioned whether God had wiped my slate clean but instead believed He had.

And I was also able to let go of a joy-robbing lie, the lie that I could never, and should never, forgive myself for what I'd done.

FORGIVE YOURSELF

When we forgive ourselves, we put into practice the gift of forgiveness we have received from God. Forgiving ourselves means letting go of guilt and shame and embracing God's grace so He can restore our hearts and minds. It's critical for us to forgive ourselves if we want to enjoy life again.

Sadly, most of us are more likely to let someone else off the hook for their mess-ups than to do that for ourselves. When it comes to our own wrongdoings, we hold ourselves forever accountable. We forgive others for terrible offenses, but we can't forgive ourselves for lesser offenses, let alone ones we deeply regret. We think we have an obligation to punish ourselves forever, even if we believe God has forgiven us.

While the Bible doesn't specifically say we are to forgive ourselves, it does address the principle. For example, in Jeremiah 31:34 God said, "And I will forgive their wickedness, and I will never again remember their sins." *The Message* says, "I'll wipe the slate clean for each of them. I'll forget they ever sinned!" You see, it's not that God can't remember our sin; He is all-knowing. It's that once He has forgiven us, He chooses not to remember or focus on our sin. When we don't forgive ourselves, we relive our sins over and over again. As Max Lucado so eloquently pointed out, "Guilt sucks the life out of our souls. Grace restores it."[2] We need to accept God's grace and give ourselves some grace too.

It took walking closely with God, staying in His Word, and a lot of prayer and faith before I was able to find freedom from the lies I had believed for so long. Lies that told me I was unworthy of God's forgiveness and He could never use me or my past for anything good. But when my heart was changed, my picture of what God looked like when I entered His throne room changed too. I no longer saw a God who was disappointed and fed up with me. Instead, I saw a God who loved me unconditionally. I saw a God who had a tender, compassionate heart and a gentle, kind face. And He was smiling—just as any loving father does when his little girl enters his presence.

As my vision of God changed, so did my vision of myself. I realized because He has forgiven me, I could forgive myself and ask Him to release me from the grip of shame, guilt, and regret.

Are you constantly bringing to mind the sins of your past and letting that rob you of the joy God wants you to have? If so, will you consider how much more joyful your life could be if you stopped doing that, beginning right now? God knows we aren't perfect, so why do we think we have to be sinless to be treasured and accepted by Him? All too often we get in a habit of listening to the lies of the one who steals, kills, and destroys, rather than to the truths of the One who gives abundant life.

You can choose which voice you listen to. The deceiver may always seem louder, but only One speaks truth: you are a precious child of God. "But God showed his great love for us by sending Christ to die for us while we were still sinners" (Rom. 5:8).

LET GO OF LIES; GRAB HOLD OF TRUTH

Although sometimes it seems easier to forgive others than to forgive ourselves, it can be done if we put our faith in the One who died for us so we don't have to live in shame and regret. By God's mercy alone, I finally came to believe God's truth that He didn't want me hanging on to my sin, much less be haunted by it every day. I realized if He had forgiven my sins, I no longer needed to be captive to them or to the enemy's lies of condemnation. If God had moved on, shouldn't I?

Shouldn't you?

Here's the thing: you and I can't pick and choose which scriptural promises to believe. Scripture tells us over and over again that God is a God who forgives *all* those who seek His forgiveness. No exceptions. His love for you is unconditional. His forgiveness is without any strings attached. If you have confessed your sin and asked God to forgive you, He has not only done so; He is thinking of it no more. And neither should you.

Although we can't completely forget the past, we can intentionally stop mentally beating ourselves up in destructive and negative ways. The past has shaped who we are, but it does not define who we are. When we accept God's forgiveness, we can be free of what haunts us and move forward in God's plan for us to enjoy and love the life we have been given.

LOVE YOUR LIFE CHALLENGE #4

Accept God's forgiveness.

Reflect

Have you been struggling with believing God could forgive you of your sins because you didn't believe you deserved it or you thought they were too big to forgive? What sin do you need to accept His forgiveness for today?

If you began to fully believe God forgives unconditionally, remembers your sins no more, and loves you, how would that change how you see yourself and how you live?

Act

If you have never received God's forgiveness or asked Him into your life, pray to accept His gift of forgiveness and salvation today. If you need to forgive yourself, set aside one morning with a blanket, your Bible, and your favorite beverage and do the following:

1. Have a deep, honest conversation with God. Close your eyes and picture Jesus sitting there with you, eyes filled with compassion and a gentle smile on His face. Let His presence sink into your heart. If you've never asked for His

forgiveness for what weighs heaviest on your heart, do so right now. Be honest. He already knows. If you have but still struggle with accepting His forgiveness, let yourself believe with your whole heart that He has forgiven—and forgotten—and vow to never bring it to mind again. Search His Word for Scriptures about forgiveness and new life to support what your heart is telling you but your mind is finding difficult for you to believe.

2. Think about what you would do differently if you were in the same position today as you were when you made your past mistake. Realize that if we learn and change from our mistakes, they have already served a purpose.

3. Give yourself time to embrace your new mind-set and stop focusing on old memories. Let yourself be proud of who you are today. You are not the same person you once were, and God will continue to transform your heart and mind as you stay grounded in the truths of His love, forgiveness, and acceptance.

Pray

Dear Jesus, You know the shame and regret I feel for the sins in my life—some from my past and some in the present. I humbly ask for Your forgiveness for all my sins. I believe You died on the cross so I could be cleansed, and I accept that gift of cleansing right now. Please help me let go of my self-condemning thoughts and the habit of reminding myself of my sins every day. Just as You have forgotten them, help me not focus on and obsess over them. Help me let them go, and free up my heart to experience more peace and joy. In Jesus' name, amen.

Smile

Choose an uplifting and wholesome movie with a strong lesson. Plan a movie night with your family or friends. Buy popcorn, candy, and drinks, or tell everyone to bring their favorite snack. Enjoy the time together and let laughter and joy fill you up more than the popcorn.

5

Forgive and Forget

Years ago when I volunteered for a position at my daughter's middle school, I had no idea of the months of heartache and frustration that would follow. I put in countless hours and had to interact with some difficult people who seemed to go out of their way to be mean to me. Every day was full of conflicts and challenges; I had to endure attacks on myself, my integrity, and sometimes my child. (One morning I even woke up to find vandalism to my home.) My heart was heavy. My mind tired. My spirit crushed. I was fed up with being treated hatefully and of feeling like a punching bag. Of feeling insecure and unaccepted. Of feeling hopeless and helpless to make things better, much less have the ability to make these women want to be friends instead of enemies. Regardless of all the good things that were accomplished and the success of our team, and despite trying to stay positive and hopeful that things would improve if I just kept doing my best, I felt like I couldn't win for losing.

As the months dragged by, I continued to stand by my commitment to serve, but I became more and more upset and resentful. Bitterness grew, stealing the peace from my heart and robbing me of the joy of living. Then one day a displeased parent approached me at practice about a situation with her child. She was fuming with hostility and anger and appeared to be on the verge of physically attacking me. To keep the confrontation from escalating further, and realizing nothing I could say would make a difference, I finally turned around and began walking toward my car while she continued yelling at me. By the grace of God alone, I somehow managed to keep from crying until she and I were no longer face-to-face, but once I got home, emotions that had been bubbling up for months spewed out like lava from an erupting volcano. I felt like a defenseless child being bullied at school, not knowing how to fix the situation. Except sadly, we were all adults.

Okay, listen up. I am the first to admit the absolute absurdity and ridiculousness of this situation. I mean seriously. I was a *volunteer* for a middle-school sports team for goodness' sake! Have mercy. Double mercy. But as absurd as my story sounds, I wonder whether it actually might sound way too familiar to you. Maybe you too have experienced the absolute absurdity and ridiculousness of power plays, emotions, politics, popularity contests, adult cliques, and women pitting women against one another. If you have, my heart goes out to you. Unkindness from other adults and even fellow believers happens everywhere—on playgrounds and in schools, in clubs and on sports teams, in classrooms and boardrooms, in workplaces and churches and neighborhoods. When other people hurt us, especially when it's intentional or make us feel as if we don't fit in, it can cause us to become bitter and angry, making it hard for us to accept, much less forgive, them.

On the day of that heated confrontation with the girl's mother, I reached a breaking point. After my emotions settled down, I spent a lot of time in reflection and prayer. As I listened for what God had to say to me, I didn't really like what He revealed. He opened my heart and eyes to the real problem; He showed me the true source of my unhappiness. It wasn't the hurtful and unwarranted behavior of others, although their actions toward me certainly caused pain. Instead, my joy and ability to love life was being robbed by all the negative emotions I was harboring against the people who were mistreating me. I was full of resentment, bitterness, and unforgiveness. No wonder I was unhappy!

The ugly truth was I didn't *want* to forgive these people—even after God pricked my heart to do so. I told myself I didn't deserve how they were treating me and they didn't deserve my forgiveness. They hadn't acknowledged their hurtful actions toward me and seemed bent on doing things that wounded me and damaged our team morale. And they most certainly had not asked me to forgive them. Nor would they ever.

But God helped me see I was the only person being punished by my refusal to forgive them. My resentment was making me feel miserable (and my dear family too, I might add). I couldn't enjoy my blessings because I was consumed with my hardships. I dreaded going to practice every day with my daughter, anxious that I would have to deal with yet another hard situation or discussion, convinced it was just a matter of time before I felt uncomfortable, unaccepted, and persecuted again. Throughout each day, I thought about the problem, talked about the problem, and worried about the problem. It was the last thing I thought about when I went to bed every night and the first thing I thought about when I woke up. As justifiable as my feelings might have been (from a human point of view), I was letting my emotions run my life and allowing them to squelch my joy.

What I have learned is this: unforgiveness keeps us in a vicious cycle of unhappiness, but we always have the power to stop the cycle.

EXTENDING FORGIVENESS

Matthew 6:15 says, "But if you do not forgive others their sins, your Father will not forgive your sins" (NIV). After God revealed the real problem to me, I knew I couldn't put off forgiveness any longer. I got on my knees and asked God to forgive me for harboring unforgiveness against others. I pled with Him to help me let go of the hurt and anger and to give me the courage to be kind to those who had hurt me, even when nothing in me wanted to and even if they didn't return that kindness. I prayed, *I forgive them, Lord*, and asked for the strength to hold on to that commitment. Then I took the hardest step of all. I prayed for all the people who had treated me with malice and unkindness as we are instructed to do in Matthew 5:44: "But I say, love your enemies! Pray for those who persecute you!"

Forgiveness wasn't easy, and I knew it would take time before my heart would soften toward those who had hurt me. I realized that forgiveness was more than uttering words but actually letting it change me from the inside out. I knew it would be a long time before the emotional wounds went away, but I also knew it was necessary to forgive, simply because I wanted to be set free. I wanted to love my life and enjoy my family and all the blessings I had. I wanted to wake up feeling happy, not discouraged and stressed. I wanted to look forward to and delight in each new day God gave me, not dread it. I didn't want to give the selfish actions of others control over whether I loved my life. In choosing to forgive, I was taking back that control.

The problem remained, but the poison did not. I set the prisoner free, and that prisoner was me.

Note: forgiving those who have wronged us or hurt us does not mean we are accepting their behavior or letting them off the hook. Rather, it means we are protecting our own hearts from the damage their behavior can cause. It does not mean we have to trust the people who have hurt us or even let them back into our lives (unless God leads us to do so).

FORGIVING FULLY

In Matthew 18:21, Peter posed a question to Jesus. He wanted to know how many times he was supposed to forgive someone who sinned against him. If you ask me, that's a valid question. If we have forgiven someone multiple times and that person continues to sin against us, who wants to keep on forgiving that individual? When our hearts get broken over and over, it's normal to put up barriers to protect ourselves from future harm. It is hard to forgive people who hurt and betray our trust time and time again—especially if they don't admit fault for their wrongdoing.

Yet that is exactly what Jesus instructed us to do. "At that point Peter got up the nerve to ask, 'Master, how many times do I forgive a brother or sister who hurts me? Seven?' Jesus replied, 'Seven! Hardly. Try seventy times seven'" (vv. 21–22 THE MESSAGE).

Say what? So we're supposed to forgive someone 490 times for sinning against us? The answer is yes. However, even when we reach 490 times (if we are keeping count, that is), we're still supposed to keep on forgiving. Jesus stated "seventy times seven" just to make the point that forgiveness is unconditional, ongoing. We are to forgive *every time* someone hurts us.

To understand why Jesus said this, it helps to keep in mind that forgiveness is a sign not of weakness but of strength. We may never know how strong we are until we have to forgive someone who doesn't ask for forgiveness or who needs it over and over again. In this passage, Jesus was teaching about the character of the believer, and Jesus' answer to Peter's question focused on character as well.

The backstory reveals that Peter's bold question was actually a little self-serving. Apparently, the Jewish rabbis of that day taught that you were to forgive a particular person up to three times. This was based on a statement in God's message to Amos: "Because of the three great sins of Damascus—make that four—I'm not putting up with her any longer" (Amos 1:3 THE MESSAGE). God forgave the enemies of Israel three times but punished them upon the fourth offense. The religious leaders taught that as the standard to follow.[1]

Some Bible commentators believe that when Peter asked whether he should forgive seven times, more than double what the religious leaders said was required, he expected Jesus to praise him for his over-the-top willingness to forgive. I wonder, too, if he was looking for commendation from Jesus in front of everyone. Jesus' answer was surely shocking and maybe even a little humbling to Peter and the other disciples: "Although they had been with Jesus for some time, they were still thinking in the limited terms of the law, rather than in the unlimited terms of grace."[2]

Jesus' point that forgiveness is born of great strength reminds me of a famous quote often attributed to Mark Twain: "Forgiveness is the fragrance that the violet sheds on the heel that has crushed it."[3] The flower was treated harshly. It did nothing to deserve that treatment, yet it endured the suffering. Even so, the flower exuded a sweet fragrance for the one who had inflicted the pain. It takes the strength of Jesus, and strong character, to be able to show love (the sweet fragrance of forgiveness) to someone who has hurt or crushed us. That is what forgiveness truly is, and this is what Jesus meant in this passage.

Forgiveness is not always easy to give, and it can't be done in our own strength, but it can be done in God's strength. Like anything worth achieving, forgiveness takes both practice and patience.

FORGIVING FAITHFULLY

When people sin against us or hurt us, we are to extend to them unlimited grace—which is exactly how God treats us. He wants us to forgive others as quickly as He forgives us. Although that seems impossible at times, especially when the hurt is great or the offense seems unforgivable, it is possible through the power of the Holy Spirit. Forgiveness doesn't change the past, but it does change our future for the better.

Romans 8:28 says, "God causes everything to work together for the good of those who love God." This is exactly what God did with the mistreatment I suffered as a volunteer at my child's school. Just as He has done many other times in my life, God transformed something the Devil meant for evil into something good.

What was the "good" that came out of this trying time in my life? I learned to accept that I cannot change other people, no matter how badly I may want to or how hard I try. I cannot change their behavior or negative opinions or actions, and I definitely cannot change their hearts. But I can always ask God to change mine.

And that is what He did. He changed my heart so I was willing and able to forgive.

Forgiveness gave me a heart full of God instead of anger and bitterness.

Forgiveness enabled me to focus on God and all the good in my life instead of staying so focused on these problems and people that my eyes could see nothing else.

The lesson I learned all those years ago also equipped me to forgive even greater offenses in the future I didn't even know were coming at the time. Offenses which could have easily resulted in unforgiveness tangling itself deep into my heart, stealing my joy, and impacting my life entirely.

FREEDOM FOR YOU

Take a moment right now to think of those whom you might need to forgive. Are there people in your life who have mistreated or hurt you? People you need to forgive—for the sake of your own heart and happiness, not theirs? Have others wronged you? Have others tormented you? Abused you in some way? Neglected you? Lied to you? Manipulated you? Been unfaithful to you? Stolen from you? Wounded you? Betrayed you? Embarrassed you?

Friend, forgive them—even if they haven't asked for it, don't deserve it, won't appreciate it, and may not recognize that they received it. Do it anyway—for *you*. Don't let unforgiveness stand between you and the ability to love your life. It may not happen overnight, but as you continue to ask God to help you forgive and let go of what hurt your heart, He will empower you.

Let forgiveness set you free and bring back your joy … today.

LOVE YOUR LIFE CHALLENGE #5

Forgive someone who hurt you and set yourself free.

Reflect

Who in your life currently, or in your past, are you purposely or inadvertently refusing to forgive? How is your refusal to forgive affecting how you interact with others, how you feel about yourself, and your overall joy?

How might your life be different if you set yourself free from the prison cell of unforgiveness?

Act

Consider the people from whom you have been withholding forgiveness, then carry out these three steps:

1. Write down the name of a person who has hurt you who you have not been willing or able to forgive.

2. Close your eyes and pray, *Lord, I forgive* [insert the person's name]. Forgiveness won't be easy, but it will be worth it. You may not feel any different at first, but over time as you continue to forgive and invite God into the process, He

will begin moving in your heart and replacing pain with peace.

3. When you're ready—and it might not happen right away—pray something positive for that person. You may not feel like it, but your willingness to pray for those who hurt you helps set your heart free.

Pray

Dear Jesus, if I have harbored unforgiveness toward someone, open my eyes to see how bitterness and resentment are affecting my joy. Give me the strength to forgive those who have wounded me. In Your name, amen.

Smile

Buy yourself a bouquet of your favorite fresh flowers and put them in a vase in your kitchen. Each time you catch a whiff of their sweet fragrance, remind yourself how loved you are by God and how forgiveness has set you free.

6

Conquer Loneliness

Not long after I became newly single, I also became an empty nester and *loneliness* began to take on a whole new meaning. At times, I was tempted to believe I would be alone forever and struggled with worrying about what my future would look like. Thankfully, I was able to recognize those thoughts for what they were—attacks from the enemy. He wants us to stay fearful and discouraged and believe nobody will love us or want to be our friend or companion, because if we're feeling consumed with loneliness, we won't be consumed with the One who never leaves our side.

Sadly, many people struggle with loneliness. In fact, according to a 2016 survey of more than two thousand Americans, 72 percent of Americans experience loneliness, and one-third of those felt lonely at least once per week.[1] Part of the reason for this percentage is too much time spent on computers and mobile devices instead of time spent face-to-face building bonds of true, intimate friendship. One assistant professor of family medicine stated that loneliness is an "invisible epidemic."[2] This epidemic is covered up by people's efforts to make it appear to the world they have more friends than they can count and life is awesome.

In addition, how we interact on social media, Facebook specifically, has a huge impact on our experience of loneliness. As of late 2017, Facebook had more than 2 billion monthly users and 1.37 billion people who logged on daily. Every minute, there were 136,000 photos uploaded, 293,000 statuses updated, and 510,000 comments posted.[3] But this type of connection does not a true friend make. True friendship means being connected deeply. Facebook and other social media platforms make it easy to feel connected to others, and some people might even boast about the number of "friends" they have, but in actuality using social media can increase our sense of loneliness. One study concluded that when Facebook users posted and shared things, liked other people's posts, or used Messenger, their sense of loneliness seemed to decrease. But for people who simply lurked on Facebook, scrolling without ever getting engaged, the opposite occurred and they felt more isolated and lonely.[4]

Loneliness is an emotion brought on as a result of feeling separated from other people, whether or not we are around others. Loneliness is more a state of mind than a state of being. It is how we feel, not where we physically are. We can be married and in the same room with our spouse and still feel completely and painfully alone. We can be at the mall among crowds of people and still feel completely alone. We can be at a high school reunion or a party, laughing and talking with dozens of friends, and still feel completely alone. We can be at a Sunday morning worship service or in a Sunday school class, surrounded by fellow believers, yet still feel utterly alone.

The word *loneliness* describes a condition of the heart and mind rather than an actual situation. Loneliness can feel like isolation and evoke deep feelings of sadness and hopelessness, causing us to feel and maybe even believe we have no friends and no one cares about us (even when we have plenty of people who do).

If someone struggles with depression or anxiety, feeling lonely can cause those problems to worsen. Like flame to fuel, loneliness ignites insecurity and despair. This is a sad reality and not how our heavenly Father wants us to think, feel, or live. God created us to be in relationships. Genesis 2:18 explicitly says we were not meant to be alone, yet sometimes that becomes our reality. Sometimes emotionally, sometimes physically.

WHAT HELPS

While there are many self-help tips available for how to deal with loneliness, I've found that nothing mends a lonely heart more than sweet words from Scripture, particularly the psalms of David.

When David wrote Psalm 142, he was running for his life, hiding in a dark cave in hopes that those who sought to kill him would not find him. Verses 1–4 read,

> I cry out to the LORD;
> I plead for the LORD's mercy.

I pour out my complaints before him
　　and tell him all my troubles.
When I am overwhelmed,
　　you alone know the way I should turn.
Wherever I go,
　　my enemies have set traps for me.
I look for someone to come and help me,
　　but no one gives me a passing thought!
No one will help me;
　　no one cares a bit what happens to me.

In this psalm, David clearly stated how he was feeling: alone. Alone with his fears. Alone with his troubles. Alone with his confusion. Alone with his joy-robbing thoughts. Alone with himself. Alone without any person who seemed to care.

But David knew exactly how to conquer his loneliness, as demonstrated in the next few verses. He turned his focus to Who was with him instead of who was not, to Whose he was instead of who he was or wasn't. Consequently, David's expressions of loneliness turned into expressions of praise and joy.

He continued:

Then I pray to you, O LORD.
　　I say, "You are my place of refuge.
　　You are all I really want in life.
Hear my cry,
　　for I am very low.

> Rescue me from my persecutors,
>> for they are too strong for me.
> Bring me out of prison
>> so I can thank you.
> The godly will crowd around me,
>> for you are good to me." (vv. 5–7)

Like David, when we feel alone, we are faced with a choice. We can focus on the One who is present with us or those who are not. Most of us have never been in a dark cave, alone and hiding from our enemies as David was. Yet loneliness can feel like a dungeon from which there is no escape. An empty place where the voice of our enemy echoes over and over again in our minds: *Nobody cares about you—or ever will. You don't have friends, because no one likes you. It is your fault you are alone. You'll always be alone.* At times this voice seems louder than any other—even God's.

Scriptures like Psalm 142 remind us that we are *never* really alone. This is good news! God is always with us, even during those times we can't sense His presence. We may think we are on our own in the world, but God always sees us, wants us, and accepts us. He is the friend we most need in our lives. He is enough to conquer our loneliness, and He wants to fill our hearts with the joy and contentment that can be found in friendship with Him. We are His beloveds, and He is our beloved friend.

Although we can and should pray for God to bring satisfying relationships into our lives, until He does, we can pray He will take away our loneliness by helping us discover a more intimate relationship with Him first.

DISCOVERING YOUR VERY BEST FRIEND

When we are feeling lonely, we are usually inclined to look to other people to quell our loneliness. But the most effective cure for loneliness is not found in relationships with people. It's far more important that we deepen our friendship with Jesus and make our relationship with Him a priority. I realize Jesus is … well … Jesus, and you might be thinking, *How can Jesus help me feel less alone when He doesn't have a physical body? Can He really take away the sadness and loneliness I feel when I'm sitting at home on a Saturday night and everyone I know has a vibrant social life except for me? When I look at social media and it seems as if I'm the only person in the world who doesn't have a strong circle of friends? When I'm watching romantic movies and my heart is aching with the desire to have someone hold me? Can Jesus really help me feel less alone and be the friend I so desperately want? How is that even possible?*

Let me tell you about Amanda, who, as a new single mom living six hours from her family and friends, discovered that Jesus could indeed meet her need for deep friendship.

Amanda and her two-year-old son lived on a meager salary, and she was forced to trust God to provide for their needs, which He miraculously did time and time again. In time she realized God was not only meeting her physical needs but He was meeting her emotional needs as well.

Many people have human companionship and digital distractions to ease the sting of the silence and pain of being alone, but Amanda had neither. She said, "All of those things are just a bandage for a festering loneliness many of us never deal with." She eventually realized that the lack of nightly distractions was a gift from God. Her son had an early bedtime, leaving her sitting alone in the house every evening. She didn't have extra money for cable or internet, so her only means of entertainment was a DVD player and some children's movies. Some evenings she had work to focus on, but she spent most of them alone with Jesus and His Word. While she never would have chosen to be a single mom with limited resources, Amanda said she recognizes that her circumstances brought her to a place where she was able to rely on Jesus to fill the emptiness in her heart.

She grew to know and love God and was content to be with Him and Him alone for the first time in her life. She learned to trust Him to meet not only her physical and financial needs but also her need for true, meaningful friendship and companionship. She discovered that He has all the traits of a true friend and she could count on Him to always be enough. Friendship with Jesus was the cure for her loneliness.

During Amanda's season of being alone, Jesus not only strengthened her faith, but He also became her confidant and helped her develop a higher standard for true companionship in any form. In time her heart mended and she was able to take the risk of trusting other people again.

It's been six years since Amanda entered her season of loneliness. She is now happily remarried to a godly man who has restored her ability to trust and love people without fear of hurt or rejection. Yet she knows that no matter what the future holds, she'll always have a best friend in Jesus.

If loneliness is keeping you from loving life, let me encourage you to build a close friendship with Jesus too.

WHY JESUS IS THE ANTIDOTE TO LONELINESS

Let's take a moment and look at the marks of true friends so you can compare the gift of earthly friendships with the friend we have in Jesus and decide for yourself whether He can quell your loneliness.

Friends Care about Us and Are Concerned about Our Lives

Good friends know when something is wrong in our lives. They can tell it in our faces, mannerisms, voices, and moods. And they care.

So does Jesus.

If you have accepted Jesus as your Lord and Savior, you are His friend. A friend is "a person attached to another by feelings of affection or personal regard."[5] In other words, a friend is someone who cares about all the details of your life because of how much he or she cares about *you*.

We see evidence of Jesus caring about us and our lives throughout Scripture, but I love how Psalm 139:1–5 brings this loving friendship to light:

> O LORD, you have examined my heart
>   and know everything about me.
> You know when I sit down or stand up.
>   You know my thoughts even when I'm far away.

You see me when I travel
and when I rest at home.
You know everything I do.
You know what I am going to say
even before I say it, LORD.
You go before me and follow me.
You place your hand of blessing on my head.

The psalmist was calling out to God and extolling the intimate friendship they enjoyed. This is the same God we can call out to today. He is a friend who not only cares about us but is also aware of every detail of our lives. He knows us better than anyone else. He knows things about us that we'd prefer people not know, including our thoughts. He even knows how many hairs we have on our heads (see Matt. 10:30). He wants the best for us and is always there to gently guide our decisions. Yet when we fail, He is there to pick us up. He loves us just the way we are but encourages us and pushes us to be all He knows we can be.

Friends Feel Compassion When We Are Hurting

Compassion is defined as "a feeling of deep sympathy and sorrow for another who is stricken by misfortune, accompanied by a strong desire to alleviate the suffering."[6] It's a feeling of such tenderness that it compels a person to deeply desire to help someone else. Jesus is the greatest example of someone who portrayed this type of compassion. During His time on earth, His compassion for others compelled

Him to perform a myriad of miracles, including raising His friend Lazarus from the dead in order to relieve the emotional suffering of Lazarus's two grieving sisters, Mary and Martha (see John 11).

Jesus not only showed compassion by alleviating physical suffering, He performed the greatest act of compassion for all humankind when He died on the cross for our sins. John 15:13 says, "There is no greater love than to lay down one's life for one's friends." There is no greater friend than Jesus, who laid down His life for me and for you.

True friends feel great compassion for us.

So does Jesus.

Friends Stay Connected

I've had some wonderful relationships with people I truly cared about and enjoyed being with, including friendships with fellow students while in college and with coworkers at former jobs. Each of these friendships once felt strong and secure, yet years, proximity, and different seasons of life made it difficult for us to stay in touch, and gradually the friendships just dissipated. Nothing happened to end these relationships, except for a lack of intentionality to stay connected.

When it comes to our friendship with Jesus, we don't have to wonder how He feels about us or whether He wants to stay connected with us. He is always present with us, always reaching out to us. If we want to experience connection with Him, we just have to make the effort to reach out to Him in return.

I learned the value of reading God's Word as a way of staying connected with God several years ago when I committed to read through the *One-Year Chronological Bible* with a group at my church. Each day I kept a journal, recording my thoughts, prayer requests, and answered prayers. This was a game changer in my faith. The Bible teaches that the primary way to hear from Jesus is through His Word and that "all Scripture is God-breathed and is useful for teaching, rebuking, correcting and training in righteousness" (2 Tim. 3:16 NIV).

Another way to reach out to God for the purpose of connection is to spend time with Him in prayer and conversation.

Oddly enough, God used a text message to help me realize that I can keep the conversation going with Him all day long because He is available 24-7. Obviously, He didn't send me an actual text message from heaven, but here's what happened. I noticed my daughter was engaged in a text conversation that had been going on for hours, if not days.

I finally asked, "Are you still talking with her?"

My daughter nodded as she continued to look down at her phone.

I said, "I just don't see how you can have that much to talk about. Doesn't the conversation ever end?"

"Nope!" she exclaimed. "We never really end the conversation or say good-bye. We just take breaks and then pick back up later where we left off."

I rolled my eyes and suggested she take a break from the conversation or I just might help her take a really long break from her phone altogether.

But my daughter's comment caused me to think about my conversations with God. How might my relationship with Him grow if I never said "Amen" to end the conversation? If I just kept the conversation going all day long, always picking back up where we left off or talking about new things?

First Thessalonians 5:17 says, "Never stop praying." In other words, never say, "Amen." Paul was urging us to pray continually, not because God requires it but because our hearts long to feel close to Him. Talking with Him throughout the day invites Him into even the smallest details of our lives.

Praying continually doesn't mean we have to stay on our knees all day or pray without ever taking a break. It doesn't mean we can never do anything else besides praying. It simply means going about our days with an attitude of prayer. To have a mind-set that God is always there, always available to have a conversation with us, always eager to hear what we have to say.

True friends intentionally try to stay connected because they want to spend time with us and keep a strong relationship going. They want to hear from us and enjoy communicating with us, no matter how much time it takes.

So does Jesus.

The more we connect with Him, the more He can connect with us. John 15:4–5 says, "Remain in me, and I will remain in you. For a branch cannot produce fruit if it is severed from the vine, and you cannot be fruitful unless you remain in me. Yes, I am the vine; you are the branches. Those who remain in me, and I in them, will produce much fruit. For apart from me you can do nothing." This

Scripture stresses the importance of "remaining" in Jesus, of living and dwelling in Him and with Him. It doesn't mean dropping in occasionally for a quick visit or "liking" Scripture-based graphics on Facebook or Instagram. It means cultivating an intimate relationship with Jesus. In this passage, Jesus is described as the vine and we are described as the branches. This illustrates what it means to remain in Him. The branch cannot live apart from the vine. We cannot live the life we are meant to live apart from a close connection with God. Deuteronomy 31:6 promises us that Jesus will never leave us or forsake us. Instead, it is usually we who leave or forsake Him. But when we're ready to reconnect, He is waiting, always, with open ears and open arms.

Friends Talk and Listen

The day my husband left will be forever etched in my memory. When he walked out and closed the door, I was left standing in the kitchen in a state of shock. Alone, confused, and despairing. I was crying, shaking, and had difficulty breathing. I didn't know what else to do in that moment except call a friend.

Amy was at her child's soccer game when she received my desperate phone call. I could hardly get intelligible words out of my mouth but managed to tell her what happened. Her immediate response was, "I'm on the way over." Amy is one of those moms, like me, who never misses a child's game, practice, performance, or banquet no matter how tired or stretched thin she feels. But on this day, she did so without hesitation. She immediately left her child's game and drove straight to my house all the way across town—in record time, I might add. She listened. She hugged. She cried along with me. She talked me down off a ledge.

I talked, and she listened. She talked, and I listened. Because that's what friends do.

So does Jesus.

In the hard months that followed, many friends stood beside me, talking and listening. I have no doubt there were times they grew weary of talking about and listening to my problems and emotional challenges, yet they stood firm in their support, compassion, and love. Those friendships played a crucial role in helping me heal and have the strength and emotional energy to keep pushing forward in faith. They were the hands and feet of Jesus in my life, and they exemplified the kind of friend we have in Him.

Jesus never grows weary of hearing about our hurts. Philippians 4:6 says, "Do not be anxious about anything, but in every situation, by prayer and petition, with thanksgiving, present your requests to God" (NIV). He wants to hear our problems and our praises. He is always there to catch our tears (see Ps. 56:8), and He hold us up when we are weak (see 2 Cor. 12:9).

And Jesus is always talking to us, whether we are listening or not. He speaks through people, sermons, music, and dreams. He speaks through promptings to our spirit, spontaneous thoughts, and, most importantly, through Scripture. If we want to hear from Him and develop a close friendship with Him, we have to spend time with Him. But rest assured—He is always talking and listening, because that's what friends do.

Friends Are Trustworthy and Faithful

We all long for friends who are trustworthy, always have our back, keep their promises, maintain our trust, and stay by our side through thick and thin. People who will never leave us, who will always be there for us and love us, no matter what.

If you're like me, you've experienced friendships that didn't meet those standards. I've had people reveal things I shared with them in confidence; I've had friends who turned their backs on me in my time of greatest need. Such betrayals sting and pierce the soul, leaving us questioning whether there really is such a thing as a true, trustworthy friend.

Oh, but there is. His name is Jesus. Jesus is exactly the kind of friend we long for: always trustworthy, always faithful, and always present.

As we invite Jesus to heal the wounds caused by broken friendships, we can learn not only to trust others again but to trust Him as well. We can embrace the truth that Jesus will never let us down or betray us, because He is completely different from anyone on earth. He is God, and nobody on earth is. He is 100 percent dependable, trustworthy, and faithful. Psalm 118:8–9 says, "It is better to take refuge in the LORD than to trust in people. It is better to take refuge in the LORD than to trust in princes." We can always count on God to be our refuge. He will never turn His back on us or betray us.

That, my friend, is the best kind of friendship we can hope for.

I know this to be true, because I have experienced His faithful friendship. On those occasions when I have felt most alone, I have always felt Jesus' presence. He was always there, even when nobody else was. When I thought everything was going bad, He would give me some reason to remember that everything was not bad, just some things were. He would prompt me to count my blessings instead of my burdens. He helped me remember that just because I was having a bad day didn't mean I was having a bad life. When I was angry or sad and wondered whether He heard my prayers, He would give me some sign to let me know I was not forgotten, overlooked, or unheard. When I felt hopeless, He would give me the strength to hang on to hope of better times. When I wondered whether I had any good traits because life and people had crushed my self-confidence, He would remind me I was fearfully and wonderfully made. On the days I've felt the weakest, He has infused me with the strength and courage I needed to keep pushing forward.

As you consider the five traits of good friends, think of how you can make friendship with Jesus a priority in your life. Be concerned with Him and His Word; let your heart feel deep gratitude for what He did on the cross for you; stay connected with Him through prayer and conversation. And most of all, stand firm in your faithfulness to Him. He wants to be your dearest friend.

LOVE YOUR LIFE CHALLENGE #6

Invite Jesus to be your best friend.

Reflect

Have you ever considered Jesus as your best friend, or have you assumed He really can't be because He is not here in the flesh? How can knowing He is always with you help you conquer feelings of loneliness?

How can pondering the traits of good and loyal friends help you embrace the friendship available in Jesus?

Act

Bow your head and invite Jesus to be your best friend. Tell Him all the reasons you need a friend today, and ask Him for open eyes to see when He is meeting your needs. How might you apply each of the five traits of being a good friend to your relationship with Jesus? Put your answers into actions today.

Pray

Lord, lately I've been feeling unseen, unwanted, unneeded, unaccepted, and all alone. But I do believe You can be the best friend I've ever had. Forgive me for not realizing the kind of friend I can have in You. Please

help me feel Your presence, especially during those times I feel most alone.
In Jesus' name, amen.

Smile

Take yourself on a dinner date. Pick your favorite restaurant and take
your Bible with you. Read it over dinner, inviting Jesus to make His
presence known and felt like never before.

7

Be a Friend

When my children were small, I had very little time outside of work for anything other than being a mommy, much less time for building and fostering friendships. Yet I desperately wished I did. Even though my life was full and I was surrounded by a host of people, I longed for some close connections with other women. While I had colleagues at work I could have a quick lunch with, lots of acquaintances at church, and was known by name to many people in our community, deep down in my heart, I knew I was lacking real friends.

I yearned for friends who would show up when I needed them, no matter how busy they were. Friends who accepted me, faults and all, without judgment. Friends who loved me and I could trust to keep confidences. Friends who listened well and laughed and cried with me. Friends with whom I could have coffee or dinner or see a movie. Friends who didn't have any agenda other than to just be a friend, who simply enjoyed being together. And I longed to be that kind of friend to someone else.

While I knew Jesus was my best friend and I could always count on Him, my heart secretly longed to have some true girlfriends, women with whom I could build close connections. That desire was met when I started praying one simple prayer.

Over a decade ago, I attended one of my first Christian women's conferences. I met a lot of new people, had some stimulating conversations, laughed a lot, and was spiritually fed. My heart was full, but not for the reasons you might think.

One of the speakers shared a powerful message laced with Scripture and encouragement about life, relationships, and faith. But it was her three-word challenge at the end of her talk that got my attention. It was simply this: *pray for friends.*

Huh? I had never thought about praying for friends before, even though I longed for them every day. It seemed like a petty, self-centered request—one that paled in comparison with all the things my family and I needed prayer for, not to mention all the things the whole wide world needed prayer for. There were so many more critical, pressing needs that my heart's desire for girlfriends just never made it onto my prayer list.

On top of that, it was hard for me to even admit I had no close friends. After all, doesn't every normal woman have a circle of close friends? If the movies and social media are to be believed, most women have friends they laugh with while eating brunch at a hip restaurant, bond with during their children's playdates, and share their deepest secrets and problems with (not to mention their clothes!). If another woman had told me she was praying for friends, I may have secretly thought it sounded a little desperate to ask God to supernaturally give you friends.

But when this sweet woman of God encouraged and challenged us to pray for God to bring friends into our lives, not only to help conquer loneliness but also to enrich our lives, I realized the truth: women need friends, yet many of us don't have them. In fact, I imagine every woman in the sanctuary that day was feeling a longing for true friendships deep in her heart, while believing she was the only one feeling that way. No matter how old we get, we all need friends—yet the older we get, the harder it can be to build new friendships, particularly when our time and energy is focused on raising a family or building a career ... or both. And especially if life or health has dealt us some hard circumstances which keep us more isolated from others, or maybe across the country from everyone we know. But there is always hope for things to change, and one Friend has the power to make change happen.

WE ALL NEED FRIENDS

In the previous chapter, we saw the importance of developing a close friendship with God and how He can strengthen and encourage us in times of loneliness. While our relationship with Him needs to be our top priority, He designed us to have relationships with people who understand us and share our interests. Our desire for close connection is part of who we are and how He knit us together. In

Proverbs 27:9, Solomon wisely said, "A sweet friendship refreshes the soul" (THE MESSAGE). His words could not be more true.

Lacking good friends can cause us to feel lonely. It can even cause us to feel envious of other women who seem to have more than their share of close friends. As we compare our lack of friends with their presumed abundance of them, our thoughts run wild. *Why does she get friends and I don't? Why is God blessing her that way and not me? Humph.* Arms crossed. Brow furrowed. *Life is so unfair.* I often had lots of these kinds of thoughts rolling through my brain all those years ago. Even while I was at the conference, I was jealous of women who walked together, laughing and appearing to know everything about each other's lives. I had a serious, joy-robbing case of friendlessness—yet I was too embarrassed to tell anyone. But my heavenly Father knew, because He knows all the desires of my heart.

PRAY FOR FRIENDS

Friendships don't happen without effort, and anything worth having is worth investing time and heart in. Truly good friends—the type of friends who warm your heart and make life full—do not usually just drop into our lives accidentally. Instead, they are often answers to prayer. They are gifts from God and treasures we can enjoy—all we have to do is ask.

Scripture tells us if we ask, we shall receive: "I tell you, you can pray for anything, and if you believe that you've received it, it will be yours" (Mark 11:24). God cares about the smallest details of our needs, including our need for friendship and companionship.

After hearing the speaker challenge us to start praying for friends, I pushed aside my pride and began doing exactly that. Day after day, month after month, I asked Him to bring women into my life who could satisfy my craving for real friendship. *God, will You please give me at least one good friend?* I set my mind on Matthew 6:8: "Your Father knows exactly what you need even before you ask him!" God knew the desires of my heart; it was okay for me to voice them in prayer. My prayers weren't desperate; they were raw and honest.

Friends didn't come popping out of the woodwork immediately or knocking on my door out of nowhere, but over time they did come.

Fast-forward one year. I began to realize that slowly but surely God was orchestrating encounters and situations in my life in answer to my prayers. Some of the relationships I had with women who had been mere acquaintances began to blossom into closer friendships. I also met new people in unexpected ways, women who shared my passions, hobbies, and interests. I started forming closer friendships with women whose hearts connected with mine through our mutual love for God.

In His perfect timing, He answered my prayers for friendship and gradually cured my case of friendlessness. One simple, humble prayer resulted in a marvelous abundance of blessings, one by one. Now, thirteen years later, many of these women God brought into my life have become my closest, dearest friends. I don't know what I'd do without them. Sometimes I wonder what I ever did to deserve such sweet friendships, but they serve as a reminder that God cares about the details of our lives. He wants us to feel satisfied so we can enjoy life abundantly.

Maybe right now you're thinking, *But I've prayed for friends in the past. God knows that is one of my deepest desires and continual prayers, but He has yet to bring anyone into my life.* If so, please don't lose heart. God's Word assures us He hears our prayers: "This is the confidence we have in approaching God: that if we ask anything according to his will, he hears us" (1 John 5:14 NIV). God always hears and always cares and is always working behind the scenes. No matter how big or small the request. Even our smallest hopes and dreams matter to God.

MAKE A MOVE

When I was struggling with not having any close friendships, it seemed to me that everyone I knew had a best friend (or many). So instead of having the confidence to call and ask someone whether she wanted to do lunch, go shopping, or grab dinner and a movie, I convinced myself all the women I knew already had enough friends and probably didn't want or need more, especially me. But the deep longing in my heart for friends remained, so one day I decided to go after what I wanted.

Sometimes we have to step outside our comfort zones so God can bring friends into our lives. We have to get out of the house and go where there are women who have the potential to become good friends. We have to make a move to achieve what our hearts desire. Here are some of the "moves" I made.

I started playing tennis with a group of women every week, even though I had never played the game before. To say I was initially a terrible player doesn't do justice to the word *terrible*. I've never been super athletic and had never held a tennis racket. Plus, trying to figure out how to keep score became an embarrassing example of my lack of math skills. But my desire for friendship was greater than my desire to look good, so I swallowed my pride and kept on playing with these women, who have now become some of my best and dearest friends. And my tennis skills have greatly improved as well!

I also began to volunteer in a ministry at my church, even though I didn't feel worthy or qualified at all. As I trusted God and followed the call on my heart, sweet relationships formed.

A few years later, I volunteered to work at a crisis pregnancy center and began counseling women, some of them young girls, who were faced with an unwanted or unplanned pregnancy. I initially struggled to make conversation and felt uncomfortable and at times nervous talking with women I had just met about serious matters of the heart and life-altering decisions. But my willingness to help others helped heal my own heart and fueled my confidence. I also met some amazing people I would never have met otherwise. I stopped being terrified to call and ask someone if she wanted to have dinner or go out for coffee. More times than not, the other woman said yes, which helped me get over my fear of asking.

We often sit around and wait for God to answer our prayers, rather than being willing to take a leap of faith and be instrumental in having those prayers answered. We don't want to move outside our comfort zones, even if good things might come of it. We do the same things we've always done, expecting God to miraculously create a different result. But if we keep waiting, doing nothing except wishing we had some friends, we may remain friendless. Why? Because sometimes God moves only when we move. Stepping out in faith invites God to step in.

If taking action sounds a bit intimidating, keep in mind that you don't have to take a huge step right off the bat, like showing up at a big gathering all alone and trying to mingle or striking up conversations with strangers at the mall or a ball game (although you could, of course!). A slow start is better than no start.

Start with some baby steps.

Be friendly. Take a risk and smile at someone you'd like to know better or compliment her outfit or something she's accomplished. If you know someone is going through a hard time, call her out of the blue and encourage her. Let her know you're thinking about and praying for her. Or send her a card, email, or text. Rather than simply "liking" someone's post on social media, make the effort to comment with something kind, playful, or encouraging. Get involved in some activities or hobbies you enjoy, even if that means going by yourself the first time, even if it means going by yourself the first time and pushing past that feeling of awkwardness. Take up a sport or join a gym, even if you have no idea what you're doing. Reach out to someone you think would make a good friend and invite her to lunch. Think outside the box and don't limit your sights to someone who is exactly like you. Be open to friendships with women who are younger or older than you or are a different ethnicity, culture, or background.

And remember to pray for God's guidance about the people you meet—for the discernment to carefully choose which ones could become good friends. Choose friends with values and goals similar to yours and who can stretch, encourage, and motivate you.

Bottom line: step outside your comfort zone and start being the friend you want to have. Pick one move; then put on your big-girl pants and do it! Keep in mind that the first time you reach out to someone is always the hardest. Once you make the first move, the second will likely seem a little bit less intimidating. And if someone declines your invitation, don't let it discourage you or force you to start thinking negative thoughts about yourself. Just try again next time or with someone else. Keep in mind there is likely a valid reason she declined, and it wasn't because you are not friend-worthy! Keep at it, keep praying, and keep trusting God hears your prayers and is working on your behalf.

The important things in life, including close friendships, require an investment of time, heart, perseverance, and trust in God. Trust God has a perfect plan for you when it comes to your need for close friends.

Just think … there is a woman out there right now who is praying for a friend like you.

LOVE YOUR LIFE CHALLENGE #7

Pray for friends.

Reflect

Are you suffering from a case of friendlessness but have been too embarrassed to even pray about it? What step can you take today to begin building a foundation for new relationships?

What kinds of things can you do to start being a friend to someone?

Act

Choose one thing you can do today to be the kind of friend you want to have.

Pray

Dear Jesus, I know You are my best friend, first and foremost. I praise You for being a friend I can always count on. But You know the desires of my heart: that I long for some close female friends. I ask You to begin to divinely orchestrate connections with the people You think belong in my life. Push me out of my comfort zone and give me the courage to make a move toward making friends, even if it feels awkward or intimidating at first. In Your holy name, amen.

Smile

Make time to call a friend or family member today who you haven't talked to in a while. Spend some time talking and catching up on each other's lives. Enjoy the gift of conversation.

8

Laugh More

We sat in the waiting room for hours, anxiously awaiting an update on my sister's surgery. When the surgeon finally entered the room, the news was not good. He explained that my sister's medical situation was worse than expected and the surgery had been more extensive than he'd anticipated. He then proceeded to tell us she would have a difficult, lengthy recovery and explained how her daily life would be forever different as a result of the surgery.

You could have heard a pin drop. As the doctor walked away, my family and I sat there without speaking, eyes filled with tears and hearts filled with worry.

But the silence ended abruptly when another patient's family entered the room, filling it with laughter and competing voices. I tried to tune them out, immersed in my worries over my sweet sister … until I heard someone boisterously say the name of Jesus several times. Fear and anxiety had been clamoring in my head but were quieted at just the mention of Jesus' name and by the sounds of this family's happy conversations. I lifted my head from my hands, curious to see who was responsible for all this joy in a cold, gloomy hospital waiting room. My eyes were drawn instantly to a beautiful elderly woman with snow-white hair in a wheelchair across the room. She was praying aloud for her husband, who was critically ill, yet she glowed with optimism and exuded an aura of encouragement, joy, and positivity.

She looked up eventually and noticed I was staring at her. I quickly averted my eyes, hoping to avoid any interaction.

To my dismay, she called out across the room in her sweet Southern accent. "Hey, honey! How are ya?"

I had no choice but to acknowledge her. I managed a pitiful smile, replying with a halfhearted, "I'm fine, thank you," hoping this would be the end of our conversation.

It wasn't.

Before I knew what was happening, she had rolled her wheelchair across the room, stopping right in front of me. I tried scooting my seat back because she was invading my personal bubble and making me just a tad uncomfortable, but my chair was already against the wall. She began telling me all about her husband, who was in surgery. I confess I was not in the mood for small talk, much less hearing a bunch of details about someone I didn't even know. Of course, I was gracious and listened and nodded as she spoke, but in truth I was not really paying attention—until something strange began to happen. As her joy bubbled out, my spirits began to lift and my burden felt lighter. Her smile stretched from ear to ear as she told me what a wonderful man her husband was. Every time she mentioned her sweet Jesus, her face lit up. I found myself hanging on her every word, wishing I could write down each hopeful, uplifting comment. Her faith-inspired, cheery disposition was a soothing balm, calming and comforting my anxious and sad heart.

When I told her about my sister's situation, this woman said something I will never, ever forget: "Honey, I hope God blesses your sister. And if He can only save one person today, I hope it is her. My husband is eighty-five years old and has lived a long and fruitful life."

Tears began to slide down my face. How could this dear woman even consider putting the life of a total stranger ahead of the life of her precious husband? And without even hesitating? How could this woman—even if it meant she would be going home alone for the rest of her life—ask God to heal my sister first and foremost? I was stunned and speechless.

She then took my hands, wrapped her cold, frail fingers around mine, and began to pray for my sister. It suddenly felt as if we were the only two people in the waiting room and had an audience of One. After she said amen, I thanked her and prayed for her husband in return. Shortly afterward, a nurse called this woman and her family, and they disappeared as quickly as they had appeared.

This frail, elderly, beautiful woman had intentionally filled her heart with the joy of Christ instead of the sadness of her circumstances. And as a result of having seen Jesus in her, I walked out of the hospital that day with a changed heart and a more cheerful spirit. We took my sister home a few days later, but the lesson I learned from this stranger about the importance of laughter and a cheerful heart—based on God, not circumstances—changed my life.

When I remember this woman, whose name I will never know, and her hope in the midst of calamity, I'm reminded of the wisdom found in Proverbs 17:22, which says, "A cheerful heart is good medicine, but a crushed spirit dries up the bones" (NIV). Her optimism, laughter, and faith-based joy were the medicine my heavy heart needed. Cheerful thoughts lead to a cheerful outlook, which leads to a cheerful heart, which leads to a positive, joy-filled life. A life we can love, even when in the midst of difficult circumstances.

CRUCIAL FOR ENJOYING THE LIFE WE HAVE

Numerous studies have demonstrated that there is a link between our attitudes and health and between our love for life and the length of our lives.

Here are some of the reasons laughter is good for us physically, mentally, and socially:

- Laughter protects the heart because it improves the function of blood vessels. Research has shown that when people laugh, the inner lining of their blood vessels expands to increase blood flow.[1]

- Laughter helps us enjoy the life we have. A study has connected the ability to laugh at ourselves to higher levels of optimism and better moods and happiness overall.[2]

- Laughter releases stress and tension. If you've ever had a good, hearty laugh, I bet you remember how good you felt afterward. Hearty laughter helps our bodies relax for up to forty-five minutes.

- It's impossible to feel angry, anxious, sad, bitter, resentful, or distressed in the midst of a good belly laugh. Laughter releases endorphins, chemicals that promote positive feelings. In fact, laughter has even been proven to temporarily relieve physical pain.

- Laughter burns calories. It's true! Ten or fifteen minutes of laughter a day can help you lose three to four pounds in a year.

- Here is probably the best benefit of all: laughter can actually help you live longer. According to a study in Norway, people with a good sense of humor lived longer than those who didn't laugh as often.[3]

Solomon's teaching in Proverbs 17:22 is undeniably true. When our lives are filled with joy and laughter, we will be healthier and happier. Laughter is something we need to incorporate in our lives on a consistent basis rather than relegate it to those times we watch a funny movie. You see, laughter is crucial for a happy heart, and joy is not optional in the life of a Christian!

A TIME FOR LAUGHTER AND A TIME FOR TEARS

But what can you do if you just don't *feel* like laughing or rejoicing? Solomon apparently understood this dilemma. In Ecclesiastes 3:4, he wrote there is "a time to cry and a time to laugh. A time to grieve and a time to dance." In other words, sometimes our emotions are negative, sometimes they are positive, and part of life is juggling our emotions well. There is an appropriate time for everything, including both happy and sad feelings.

When life throws you curve balls, tragedy, and unexpected hardships, grief and tears are healthy, appropriate, and exactly what is called for. There will always be times when life stinks and everything seems to be going wrong. Times when you don't feel like laughing and joy seems to be a thing of the past. Times when suffering of some sort is taking place, whether it be broken hearts, broken dreams, or broken bodies. There will also be times for laughter and dancing. Solomon wants us to understand that it's okay to feel both ways, but we never want to let our grief steal our joy completely. Because we always have God's joy within reach, we don't ever have to let our circumstances, no matter how dire, completely confiscate our happiness and joy.

When we allow ourselves to laugh, even during hard times, joy returns. Charlie Chaplin, the silent-film comedian, is reported to have said, "A day without laughter is a day wasted."[4] I wholeheartedly agree! Find at least one reason to smile today, and let that smile turn into laughter and rejoicing.

Sometimes that simply means not taking yourself too seriously.

DON'T TAKE YOURSELF TOO SERIOUSLY

While on vacation many years ago, my traveling companions and I were sitting at the gate of an international terminal at the airport, waiting for our flight. This airport was much different from the airports I was used to, with their carpeted floors, clean restrooms, and numerous shops and places to eat. Instead, this airport was old and unkempt. The carpet looked as though it had been months since it had been vacuumed. It was full of holes from years of wear and tear and neglect. The tile floors were smudged and cracked. The leather seats throughout the terminal had many with rips and holes. The air-conditioning was also not working, since it was as hot inside the terminal as it was outside on the tarmac.

I excused myself to visit the restroom before we boarded the plane, only to discover it was not up to "normal" standards either. I layered the toilet seat with multiple layers of toilet paper in an effort to protect myself from germs. After washing my hands, I left the restroom and walked back to my gate. Along the way it seemed as if a few people were giving me an odd look, but I assumed it was just my imagination. But when I reached the gate and approached a group of fellow passengers, they started snickering. What was going on? I looked around, trying to figure out what was so funny. I didn't understand why people were laughing—until my friend clued me in. I turned around and saw the cause: a long piece of toilet paper trailed behind me.

It would have been bad enough if the toilet paper was stuck to my shoe. Instead, it was stuck in the back of my shorts. Apparently, in my haste to leave the dirty restroom, I had tucked a long piece of toilet paper from the seat into my clothing. When I say "long," I mean six to seven feet long. That's longer than the train on most wedding gowns, for pity's sake! And here I had been walking around, without a clue.

When I realized what had happened, my cheeks got hot and red. I snatched the flowing paper from my clothing, balled it up, and tossed it into the nearest trash can while trying to ignore the people buckled over in hushed hysteria.

Yet despite my embarrassment, I couldn't help but laugh—and I have been laughing about it ever since. Even as I am writing this story, recalling all the little details, I can't stop chuckling.

But here's the thing: I could have handled that situation quite differently. I could have given dirty looks and made snide remarks to the strangers who were pointing and laughing at me. I could have felt anger toward all the people who failed to have the common courtesy to inform me of my toilet paper train as I passed them on my trek back from the restroom. I could have been upset with my friends, who showed me no mercy. Every time they looked at me, they started laughing and giggling. I could have felt humiliated and embarrassed for the rest of the trip. But instead of getting mad and letting this situation ruin my attitude, my day, and maybe my relationships, I joined in the laughter. And I have to confess that had it happened to someone else, I'm sure I would have been laughing too.

Life is full of opportunities to choose how we're going to act or react when we have done something embarrassing or made a mistake. How we choose to think about those situations drives our emotions, whether good or bad. If we have made a commitment to live with joy and laughter despite our circumstances, we are better equipped to handle these touchy situations with a light heart and a smile—even if the joke's on us.

It's one thing to laugh at a hilarious show, a joke, or someone else's mishap. But when we are able to laugh at ourselves, it demonstrates that we can keep pride in check, be reflective, and remain self-aware. We all say things we wish we could unsay. We all have things we wish we could change about ourselves, such as a personality quirk or a habit. All of us have mistakes we'd like to undo or embarrassing moments we wish we could erase from memory. Either we can be grumpy about those things and let them steal our joy and dampen our positive attitudes, or we can accept them as part of who God made us to be and part of the lives He gave us. Life is not meant to be taken so seriously that we can't enjoy living it.

CHOOSE JOY

How much more could you enjoy the life you've been given if you tried to find a reason to laugh and smile every day? Don't just think about it—make a conscious effort today to laugh out loud and smile more.

If you begin to laugh at yourself when you make a mistake; if you smile when problems arise, trusting that God is in the midst of the situation; if you purposely look for reasons to feel joy even when life is hard; if you try to see the good side of things instead of the bad; if you set aside time to watch a movie that makes you laugh, how much do you think your happiness level would rise? I dare say—a lot! Be brave and take it one step further. Bring to mind a time you were embarrassed or did something comical. Then share it with somebody else. Let that person know you've never told anyone else about it but wanted to bring a smile to his or her face, as well as to yours. Laughter is sweet medicine for a downhearted person.

I believe the elderly woman I told you about at the beginning of the chapter made a conscious, faith-based decision to choose joy and laughter. Her deep faith in God enabled her to be full of hope and concern for others, even in the middle of her husband's medical crisis. Her cheerful personality didn't just happen, and it didn't just happen overnight. I imagine she had spent a lifetime focusing on her faith and choosing joy and laughter in the midst of hard times. I wonder how many hearts she has encouraged and inspired over the years with her warmth and kindness. I suspect she was in her mideighties, yet her demeanor, skin, mannerisms, and smile made her seem much younger. I am confident that her overall health and happiness was due to her ability to tap into the gift of laughter and due to her positive attitude and cheerful, joy-filled heart.

Philippians 4:4 says, "Always be full of joy in the Lord. I say it again—rejoice!" Notice it doesn't say, "Be full of joy if the situation is good." It says, "Always be full of joy," in the good times and the bad. In the times you succeed and the times you fail.

In faith …

- You can always be full of joy, even when life is not going the way you wanted.

- You can always be full of joy, even when you do something embarrassing.

- You can always be full of joy, even when you experience loss or heartache.

- You can always bring joy to others through the way you choose to live. In fact, you have the power to change someone's life by simply choosing to smile.

During those times life gives you good reason not to feel joyful, during difficult seasons when laughter seems a thing of the past, rest assured you can choose joy. Laughter and joy are still in us, even when life is hard. We just have to open the door to let joy prevail instead of misery.

Always be full of joy in the Lord, and give yourself permission to laugh every day.

LOVE YOUR LIFE CHALLENGE #8

Start a habit of smiling and laughing every day.

Reflect

When is the last time you had a really good belly laugh? How did you feel afterward?

Have you accidentally let laughter and humor become a thing of the past? How did this happen? What can you do to feel joyful again or draw more laughter into your life?

Act

Do something to foster laughter in your life today. Watch a clean stand-up comic routine, get together with a friend to tell her about an embarrassing moment, spend time with a friend who exudes happiness or has the ability to make you laugh, tell a joke to a coworker, or start writing down things that kids, nieces, or nephews say or do that are too humorous to forget. And remember to smile as often as possible.

Pray

Jesus, thank You for the gift of laughter. It not only makes me feel better, but it keeps me healthy too. I have been missing the joy of laughter in my life as a result of letting my circumstances stand in the way of my happiness. Open my eyes to see all the reasons I have to smile and laugh every day. In Your name, amen.

Smile

Watch a movie that makes you laugh and feel happy, even if it's one you've seen a dozen times. Sometimes being reminded of how good it feels to laugh refreshes our entire mind and spirit and opens the door for positive habits to permanently take root.

9

Turn Complaining into Praising

When my daughter Kaitlyn was just a toddler, she became annoyed with her big sister, Morgan. Kaitlyn toddled over to me with a frustrated look on her precious little face, raised her eyebrows, flailed her hands in the air, and began to whine profusely. Granted, she didn't use actual words (at least words I could understand!), just jumbled sounds, but there was absolutely no question she was doing everything in her toddler power to have a serious case of whine. Her tone, facial expression, hand movements, the way her voice went up and down and lingered on certain "words," and the way she dragged out the end of her "sentences" all signaled she was one unhappy camper. Kaitlyn had heard her sister whine (and probably her mom too), and even though she didn't have the words to express her frustrations, she knew exactly what whining sounded like. Complaining apparently

just comes naturally to us, since we start complaining about as soon
as we can talk. But that is not what God intended.

Okay, I'll just come out and say it. I admit to being a complainer
when things aren't going my way. We all do it, and it's probably one
of the most tolerated and overlooked sins. At our jobs we complain
about the workload, the stress, the extra hours we have to put in, and
the people we have to work with. We complain about the messes the
kids leave everywhere. We complain to our friends about our spouse
in the hopes of getting confirmation on our opinion.

We complain when our plans go haywire—it's raining the day
we planned to go to the beach, or it's too hot and sunny the day we
wanted to take our kids to the amusement park. We complain that
heavy snow caused our children's schools to close, and when school
is back in session, we complain about having to wait in the long
carpool line. We complain about getting caught in a traffic jam and
about getting a speeding ticket when traffic is moving. We complain
when our favorite television show gets canceled. We are always complaining about what other people are doing that we don't like. And
on and on and on it goes.

God didn't create us so we could be full of complaints. He
designed us to be full of praise for Him. Yet it's easy to let negativity
become part of who we are. If we're not careful, complaining can
develop into a habit that is hard to break and kills our joy.

In the book of Philippians, Paul made it clear we can choose joy,
even in the midst of problems and difficulties, and taught how to
avoid developing a habit of complaining.

FOCUS ON GOD INSTEAD OF CIRCUMSTANCES

In Philippians 1, Paul wrote:

> Whatever happens, conduct yourselves in a manner worthy of the gospel of Christ. Then, whether I come and see you or only hear about you in my absence, I will know that you stand firm in the one Spirit, striving together as one for the faith of the gospel without being frightened in any way by those who oppose you. This is a sign to them that they will be destroyed, but that you will be saved—and that by God. For it has been granted to you on behalf of Christ not only to believe in him, but also to suffer for him, since you are going through the same struggle you saw I had, and now hear that I still have. (vv. 27–30 NIV)

In this passage Paul was encouraging the Philippians to stand firm in their faith against external conflicts, particularly when people were trying to persecute them or silence their teaching of the gospel. He instructed them to conduct themselves in a manner worthy of God and to be united in their faith, serving one God and one purpose. He also encouraged them not to be intimidated by their enemies.

Then in Philippians 2 he said, "Do everything without grumbling or arguing" (v. 14 NIV). Paul was gently yet firmly instructing the Philippians not to grumble and fuss "so that you may become blameless and pure, 'children of God without fault in a warped and crooked generation.' Then you will shine among them like stars in the sky as you hold firmly to the word of life" (vv. 15–16 NIV). He wanted them to know that when we complain about anything, whether it is a person or a circumstance, we are essentially casting a shadow on God's reputation.

We see an example of Paul heeding his own advice in 2 Corinthians 7: "When we arrived in Macedonia, there was no rest for us. We faced conflict from every direction, with battles on the outside and fear on the inside" (v. 5). *The Message* puts it this way: "We couldn't settle down. The fights in the church and the fears in our hearts kept us on pins and needles. We couldn't relax because we didn't know how it would turn out." The struggles Paul endured were different from yours or mine, but he was full of anxious and negative thoughts, just as we often are when we face problems and difficulties. He was tired and frustrated by all the problems, which seemed unending. But despite the challenges he encountered, Paul didn't complain in this passage or blame others for his problems— even though he had more than sufficient reasons to complain and blame. Instead, he turned this prime opportunity to whine into a prime opportunity to praise God. Instead of feeling sorry for himself or getting angry at God for allowing him to be in that situation, Paul put his focus on God and His goodness.

In 2 Corinthians 7:6, Paul wrote, "But God, who comforts the downcast, comforted us by the coming of Titus" (NIV). Rather than complaining and grumbling against God, Paul began thinking of something encouraging. Despite all the fears, unknowns, and frustrations he was facing, he intentionally chose to think of something that made him happy.

In Philippians 2:18, Paul told us to "be glad and rejoice" (NIV). He purposely decided to eliminate discontentment and grumbling from his thoughts and replace them with thoughts of joy. He wanted to feel glad and praise God no matter what, and he wanted others to experience that too.

COMPLAINING VERSUS LAMENT

Complaining is essentially accusing God of not being fair, of not doing things as He should. As we see in Exodus 16, when we complain, we are really complaining against God. In this passage, the Israelites were complaining about their lives in the wilderness and not having enough food to eat. They said, "If only the LORD had killed us back in Egypt.... There we sat around pots filled with meat and ate all the bread we wanted" (v. 3). Moses let them know they were complaining against God: "The LORD will give you meat to eat in the evening and bread to satisfy you in the morning, for he has heard all your complaints against him. What have we done? Yes, your complaints are against the LORD, not against us" (v. 8).

If nothing in your life has been going as you would like, I bet you too have found yourself complaining or whining. That's okay, as long as you do it privately in conversation with God. He wants us to come to Him with our problems and complaints, instead of spreading negativity to those around us or letting complaining and negative talk become a habit. Psalm 142:2 says, "I pour out my complaints before him and tell him all my troubles." This is considered one of the psalms of lament. The book of Psalms contains examples of how we are to express ourselves to God—how to praise and worship our God and how to talk with God about the things in our lives we don't like or wish could be changed. Around one-third of the psalms are laments. They are meant to teach us how to complain to God in a way that glorifies, praises, and expresses trust in Him. They let us know we're not the only ones who have problems and concerns or the only ones who have reason to complain. They show us that God cares about us, loves us, and understands what we're going through. He wants us to tell Him how we feel, and He already knows our thoughts before we even speak them aloud or in prayer (see Ps. 139:4).

It's okay to feel like life is treating us unfairly and to desperately want God to do something about a problem we're facing. We all feel that way occasionally. It's okay to feel sad, to mourn, or to grieve in the face of loss and disappointment. It's okay to not love all the frustrating, hurtful, or annoying things that happen to us and to even feel a little (or a lot) disgruntled. In fact, it's okay to not be in love with our lives every moment. All these are natural, human emotions. But it's not okay to stay stuck in a negative, whiny mind-set and for dissatisfaction to become a habit, since complaining opens the door for the enemy to wiggle his way into our hearts. That's why, when life is hard, we must fight for joy.

FIGHT FOR JOY

Either we can whine and complain about our problems, enabling our feelings to hold our joy hostage and our circumstances to blind us to God's goodness, or we can ask God for the ability to rejoice and love life, even when times are hard. Even when we don't feel like it. Even when we have to fight for our joy. God longs to answer this prayer, bless us, and give us joy and hope. He wants to transform our hearts and minds so we can live each day rejoicing and praising Him instead of whining and complaining.

When our perspective changes, we will engage with God in hopeful, positive conversations, just as Paul encouraged us to do. When we pray through the lens of God's perspective, instead of whining about how things appear from our perspective, we open the door for God to fill our hearts with joy, even in the hardest of seasons.

When we find ourselves in extremely hard times, people usually understand if we're grumpy and downhearted, which can make us feel justified in living with an unhappy mind-set. But Philippians 4:4 instructs us to rejoice in all seasons: "Always be full of joy in the Lord. I say it again—rejoice!" I especially love how *The Message* translates this passage:

> Celebrate God all day, every day. I mean, revel in him! Make it as clear as you can to all you meet that you're on their side, working with them and not against them. Help them see that the Master is about to arrive. He could show up any minute!…

Instead of worrying, pray. Let petitions and praises shape your worries into prayers, letting God know your concerns....

Summing it all up, friends, I'd say you'll do best by filling your minds and meditating on things true, noble, reputable, authentic, compelling, gracious—the best, not the worst; the beautiful, not the ugly; things to praise, not things to curse. (vv. 4–9)

Life is just too precious to spend every day being grumpy, miserable, and hopeless. Who wants to live that way?

I certainly don't. And I bet you don't either. Neither did my friend Lori. She learned firsthand what we choose to think about determines how we live.

There was a time in Lori's life when she struggled with feeling negative, bitter, and ungrateful *every single day*. It was a difficult season. Instead of praising God and fighting for joy, she says she did a lot of grumbling to and against God. Her heart had very little joy—until the day she decided to change that.

During this time, Lori lived with her dad, who had Alzheimer's. Even before his diagnosis and the progression of his disease, he had been a very negative man, but the disease compounded his negativity, making him an extremely difficult person to care for and live with. To make matters worse, Lori suffers from rheumatoid arthritis and her disabilities prevent her from working, which meant she couldn't afford to buy her own home. Although she'd always dreamed of being a happily married wife and mother, that was not her story. When she was in college, Lori was raped and got pregnant as a result. She kept the baby and became a single mom. As a result of the unfairness of what had happened to her, Lori had a hard time seeing the good things God had done in her life, because her life had turned out to be so different from what she wanted or felt she deserved.

But living with and taking care of her father, who was chronically negative and had a toxic habit of complaining, opened her eyes to the toll that complaining and grumbling takes on us and other people. She began to pray for the Lord to show her own heart to her and reveal to her the sins she needed to confess and the habits she needed to change. God showed her that grumbling and complaining not only had become a habit and part of her personality but were also causing her stress and negatively affecting her health. Rather than become like her dad, Lori decided she was going to start praising God, no matter what and despite her circumstances.

As she worked toward changing her heart, Lori started journaling and writing down at least five things she was thankful for every day. She spent time reading God's Word and chose to believe His promises were meant for her. She listened to sermons that taught about how powerful our thoughts are and how to break free from the bondage of complaining. She wrote out several Bible verses that spoke about being in a season of difficulty and what God promises those who are in hard situations. She also looked up verses that opened her eyes to how much God despises complaining.

Although Lori's circumstances are still the same, her heart and mind are not. She is closer to God and happier and more content with her life than ever. Even so, it's a daily commitment for her to fight for joy and remember to praise instead of complain. Lori fights for her joy every day because she wants to live a blessed life not a cursed life, lacking joy.

TURN THINGS AROUND

Sweet friend, Jesus came so we could all enjoy the promise of eternal life after death but also so we could enjoy abundant life on this earth (see John 10:10). You don't have to live an unhappy life just because your circumstances are unhappy, and you don't have to let the habit of whining and complaining become part of your personality. Instead, focus on praising God rather than cursing your circumstances, and joy will follow. While it is true that Jesus came to give us the gift of abundant life, He doesn't force us to take the gift. We must choose it.

So how do we fight for joy? By doing some of the things Lori did so God can work on and transform our hearts. We fight for joy when we choose to have regular quiet times of prayer and Bible reading. We fight for joy when we choose thankfulness by writing down at least five things we are grateful for before going to bed each night.

It's never too late to start living differently. If you weren't happy with yesterday, then choose to be happy with today. Change the way you are thinking. Turn your grumbling into praising. Ask God to make you aware when you complain so you can capture that thought and replace it with a grateful one. If you want to love life again, I encourage you to grab hold of the joy found in Christ at all costs. Always remember that our troubles are not permanent. They too shall pass. But joy helps us keep going until they do.

If you're willing to fight for it through faith, joy can be yours every single day.

LOVE YOUR LIFE CHALLENGE #9

Commit to developing a lifestyle of praise.

Reflect

When you pray, do you typically whine to God about your problems, or do you thank Him for your blessings? Do you need a better balance between sharing your complaints with Him and praising Him for all He's done?

What habit can you implement to start turning around thought patterns of complaining?

Act

Place a rubber band on your wrist. Each time you catch yourself complaining or whining about something, whether to yourself, someone else, or God, snap the rubber band and then move it to your other arm. This will help you become more aware of when you complain which can help you change your habit of complaining into a habit of praising instead. Each time you move the rubber band to the other arm, praise God for something good in your life, no matter how small.

Pray

Dear Jesus, I have a habit of complaining to others and even to You. Help me be more aware of when I am complaining. Rather than complain, help me talk with You about my problems and challenges in a way that gives You praise and honors the fact that I can trust You with my life. Thank You for who You are and for all You've done for me and blessed me with. In Your name, amen.

Smile

Buy someone you know a small gift "just because." Hand deliver it and share in the recipient's joy as he or she opens the gift. You'll bring a smile to his or her face, and to your own.

10

Stop Stressing over the Future

Sherri had been married to Harry for twenty-eight years when her world came crashing down. Because of circumstances beyond her control, many of which were unknown to her, Harry had been struggling emotionally and spiritually. So much so that he took his own life. The date is forever etched in her memory: August 18, 2013.

The shock was overwhelming. Her unbearable grief was intensified by the heartache her three young daughters were experiencing because of the unexpected and tragic loss of their daddy. Although the journey was long and hard, Sherri held on to the Lord's promises with all her might. She spent time in God's Word and soaked up the pastor's sermons on Sunday mornings. She leaned on Scripture verses for strength, such as "Do not be grieved, for the joy of the LORD is your strength" (Neh. 8:10 NASB) and "He will be the stability of your times" (Isa. 33:6 NASB).

It would have been understandable if Sherri had chosen to respond differently. Many people do. When life feels unfair or tragedy comes their way, many people get angry at God for what He has allowed to happen; some assume the future will forever be bleak and hopeless, and they adopt a doom-and-gloom mentality. Others are consumed with stress and anxiety, wondering "when the other shoe will drop." And some even turn their backs on their faith.

But Sherri did none of that.

She relied on God's strength to keep her from obsessing and stressing over the future. She chose to trust He was in control and to walk daily by faith alone—even though she had no idea how she would support herself or her family in the years to come as a stay-at-home mom. She chose to fix her thoughts on God so she wouldn't get stuck on worrying over the unknowns in her future. She invited God to hold her up and carry her forward—and He did exactly that in miraculous ways.

Sherri enrolled in a master's degree program with the goal of getting a degree in counseling. Guess when her first day of class was? August 18, 2014, the one-year anniversary of her husband's suicide. God had a perfect plan for redeeming that day, one Sherri had never anticipated.

Fast-forward three years. On August 18, 2017—four years to the day from when she lost her husband—Sherri finished her internship and completed her master's degree in counseling. Not only did God walk with her through the most heart-wrenching season of her life, but He also had a plan and purpose for her and her pain, just as we're told in Jeremiah 29:11: "'For I know the plans I have for you,' says the LORD. 'They are plans for good and not for disaster, to give you a future and a hope.'"

Four years earlier, Sherri had wondered whether she would ever love life again. She had no idea what her future held, but God did, and He was working behind the scenes to orchestrate miracles that only He could do. He had already planned her future so precisely it was even down to the exact date she would begin and complete her studies—the one day of the year that held greater meaning in Sherri's heart than any other day. God miraculously transformed that day, which had once symbolized the end of life as Sherri knew it, to become a symbol of new life and the power and divine intervention of a perfect, sovereign God. God is always directing our lives. We just have to trust Him and live with open eyes to see His miraculous handiwork.

Rather than let stress and worry consume her, Sherri intentionally chose to trust in God and find peace in Him, no matter what. She kept taking the next step, day after day, loving life despite life, while trusting that God was leading the way and opening doors to things she never even imagined she would be doing. Most importantly, God healed her heart in ways she at one time thought were impossible.

Sherri said, "God allowed me to start and finish something on a date that needed a positive associated with it. Starting and finishing my degree on this date is no accident, and I don't dismiss the significance of it. I'm amazed that with all the things the Lord does, He also coordinates calendars. Jesus really is big enough."

As I like to say, there are no such things as coincidences, only God-incidences, because God is always in control. He is big enough to handle our current problems and every day the future holds. Our future is already planned out and prepared by Him in ways we could never even dream of.

Are you struggling with fears of your own today, wondering if God can provide in the ways you need Him to? It's hard to stop looking at our limitations and situations, trying to anticipate what is going happen, and trust that God will somehow supernaturally work things out for us. But *hard* doesn't mean "impossible." You can do hard things by making the decision to believe not only that God *can provide* but that He *will.* Believing God is always working behind the scenes enables us to let go of stress and worry and to love our lives because "we know that for those who love God all things work together for good" (Rom. 8:28 ESV).

A STORY OF GOD'S CARE AND PROVISION

In the days after my divorce became final, as I struggled to ward off a doom-and-gloom mentality and often felt trapped in the eye of a tornado swirling with worry and hopelessness, one Bible story in particular helped me believe that God had my life, my problems, and my future all figured out even though I didn't. But most of all, it helped me embrace God's promises that He is our provider and protector and we can put all our trust and faith in those promises. This story holds proof of that divine ability to provide for us and protect us. And it demonstrates that God can heal and restore what we think is unmendable, unfixable, and unredeemable.

The book of Ruth tells the story of how Naomi and her husband were forced to leave their hometown of Bethlehem and move to a foreign country, Moab, because of a severe famine in Israel. Sometime after they had relocated, Naomi's husband died, leaving her a widow with two sons. Her sons married Moabite women, Ruth and Orpah. After about ten years, both of Naomi's precious sons died, leaving her with her two daughters-in-law, overwhelming grief and worry, and the belief that her future was doomed.

In the aftermath of her losses, Naomi came to believe that God was unfair to her. She said, "Don't call me Naomi; call me Bitter. The Strong One has dealt me a bitter blow. I left here full of life, and GOD has brought me back with nothing but the clothes on my back. Why would you call me Naomi? God certainly doesn't. The Strong One ruined me" (Ruth 1:20–21 THE MESSAGE). Naomi was angry at God and believed He had "ruined" her. She was discouraged and certain nothing good could ever come of her life. She had lost everything dear to her; she was so angry she actually changed her name to "Bitter." Naomi convinced herself that her life was terrible and the potential for a joyful future had been destroyed. She believed things were not going to change for the better, the life she had known was over, and she could never love her life again.

I can remember times I have felt exactly like Naomi. Maybe you can too. Maybe you are feeling that way right now. If so, read on. The book of Ruth gave me hope, and I believe it will give you hope too. Our lives may be difficult at times, but they are never, ever doomed. God can and will provide for our needs, whatever they are, just as Paul assured us in Philippians 4:19: "And this same God who takes care of me will supply all your needs from his glorious riches, which have been given to us in Christ Jesus."

We can rest assured that God is preparing our future, one holy step at a time. I love this story because it offers us a glimpse of God working behind the scenes to ensure that Naomi and Ruth were protected and provided for. He had a divine plan in place. These grieving, impoverished women just didn't know it yet. The same is often true for us. We can't see what lies ahead, but God always has a plan for meeting our needs and taking care of us.

The story continues: "So Naomi returned from Moab, accompanied by her daughter-in-law Ruth, the young Moabite woman. They arrived in Bethlehem in late spring, at the beginning of the barley harvest" (Ruth 1:22). Interesting. Do you think it was pure chance that the spring barley harvest was beginning upon their arrival in Bethlehem? Absolutely not. God had divinely orchestrated the timing of every detail of Ruth's and Naomi's lives: the move to Moab, the deaths of Naomi's husband and sons, and Naomi and her daughter-in-law's return to Bethlehem. The timing was part of God's plan to meet Naomi's and Ruth's needs, physically and emotionally.

Ruth 2 goes on to tell how Ruth swallowed her pride and gathered the grain stalks left behind as the harvesters worked. It must have taken great humility for her to gather the scraps.

It is at this place in the story where we see God's plan for protection and provision beginning to play out. "Then Boaz asked his foreman, 'Who is that young woman over there? Who does she belong to?'" (v. 5). Then Boaz told Ruth, "I have warned the young men not to treat you roughly. And when you are thirsty, help yourself to the water they have drawn from the well" (v. 9). Ruth may have been worried that her presence in the midst of so many men would make her vulnerable to being harassed, attacked, or even sexually harmed. But God had a plan to protect her, and here we see it become a reality.

At mealtime Boaz offered Ruth food and allowed her to dip her bread in the sour wine. He gave her roasted grain, and she ate until she was stuffed and still had food left over. He then told his workers, "Let her gather grain right among the sheaves without stopping her. And pull out some heads of barley from the bundles and drop them on purpose for her. Let her pick them up, and don't give her a hard time!" (vv. 15–16). At the end of the day Ruth had an entire basket of grain, which she took home to give Naomi (vv. 17–18). God had a plan to provide for their sustenance, and here we see that plan playing out.

The book of Ruth ends with Boaz purchasing Naomi's land and marrying Ruth, securing both of their futures. God had a plan to provide for their financial and physical needs, and here we see those provisions becoming a reality as well.

But He didn't stop there. Ruth and Boaz eventually had a son (see 4:13). So not only did Ruth get a son, but Naomi got a grandson to care for and love and call her own (see v. 16). Her grandson couldn't replace the sons she had lost, but surely that precious little boy filled the empty places in her heart with a new joy and purpose for living. God had a plan to meet Naomi's emotional needs and heal her heart, and again we see His plan becoming a reality. As it turns out, their worrying, fretting, and feeling life was over was all for naught.

As I write these words and think about how God orchestrated such unbelievable protection and provision for Ruth and Naomi, I am moved to tears. God orchestrated miracles long before they knew they would need them. Then He brought His plans to fruition at the exact time Ruth and Naomi thought all was lost. Divine intervention. Unbeknownst to them. Despite bitterness or lack of faith. It's a beautiful story of God's ability to provide, protect, and restore what we think is beyond restoration. But tears are also falling because, as one of God's girls, I too have experienced the reality of His provision and protection.

It's one thing to hear stories about how God meets people's needs in miraculous ways, whether from the Bible or in everyday life. But it's an entirely different thing when He miraculously intervenes for us. All I can say is, wow! (I'll tell you more about how He did this for me in a few pages.)

THE DIFFERENCE BETWEEN WORRY AND CONCERN

Perhaps you are thinking, *I really am trying to trust God and not worry, but I don't want to be naive or have my head in the sand either.*

Aren't there things we should be concerned about because there is something we can do about them? This is a valid question and one I have asked too. Obviously, we can't go through life completely unconcerned about anything, but keep in mind there is a big difference between being genuinely concerned about something in the present and being fretfully worried about what might happen in the future.

Concern focuses on a problem that needs our current attention and we can do something about. For example, we should be concerned that our children have the school supplies they need, are dressed appropriately for the weather, and have a safe ride to school. We should be concerned about our aging parents, that they are well cared for and safe. We should be concerned about working diligently to meet an important deadline and doing our best at work.

While concern is usually focused on others and motivates us to take some kind of positive action, worry doesn't do either of those things. In fact, just the opposite. Worry is self-centered, as it's usually focused on how a certain situation is going to affect us. We worry something will turn out badly, a "what-if" or worst-case scenario will come true, and the consequences will negatively affect our lives. Rather than motivating us to take positive action and compelling us to move forward with good intentions and actions like genuine concern does, worry often paralyzes us, especially when it is fueled by fears of what might happen in the future … things over which we have no control. Things only Jesus knows and has authority over. Things no amount of worry will ever solve or prevent.

That's why Jesus tells us to leave our worries with Him.

LET JESUS WORRY ABOUT TOMORROW

In the Sermon on the Mount, Jesus reassured us that He is sufficient to provide for all our needs in every way imaginable.

> Therefore I tell you, do not worry about your life, what you will eat or drink; or about your body, what you will wear. Is not life more than food, and the body more than clothes? Look at the birds of the air; they do not sow or reap or store away in barns, and yet your heavenly Father feeds them. Are you not much more valuable than they? Can any one of you by worrying add a single hour to your life?
>
> And why do you worry about clothes? See how the flowers of the field grow. They do not labor or spin. Yet I tell you that not even Solomon in all his splendor was dressed like one of these. If that is how God clothes the grass of the field, which is here today and tomorrow is thrown into the fire, will he not much more clothe you—you of little faith? So do not worry, saying, 'What shall we eat?' or 'What shall we drink?' or 'What shall we wear?' For the pagans run after all these things, and your heavenly Father knows that you need them. But seek first his kingdom and his righteousness, and all these things will be given to you as well. Therefore do not worry about tomorrow, for tomorrow will

worry about itself. Each day has enough trouble of
its own. (Matt. 6:25–34 NIV)

I return to this passage time and again for hope and reassurance
that God is still on His throne, He truly is big enough to handle
anything I come up against, and I can trust in His ways 100 percent.

Worry over the future—or anything—is not good for us in any
way. Worrying negatively affects our mental and physical health and
can actually make us age more quickly and be more susceptible to
depression.[1] It is a pointless, joy-robbing, and life-stealing habit.

Whenever we feel stressed (worry and anxiety are always at the
root of stress), our bodies think we are in danger. God didn't create
us to live in a chronic state of worry, and when we do, our bodies
react as if they are being threatened. Stress hormones like adrena-
line and cortisol begin coursing through the bloodstream. This can
cause heavier breathing, sweating, an elevated heart rate, and even
insomnia.[2]

An article in *Harvard Women's Health Watch* says this about the
negative and life-threatening effects of worry, fear, and anxiety:

> There's growing evidence of mutual influence
> between emotions and physical functioning....
> Nearly two-thirds of the estimated 40 million
> adults with anxiety disorders are women.... Anxiety
> has been implicated in several chronic physical ill-
> nesses, including heart disease, chronic respiratory
> disorders, and gastrointestinal conditions. When

> people with these disorders have untreated anxiety,
> the disease itself is more difficult to treat, their
> physical symptoms often become worse, and in
> some cases they die sooner.[3]

Worrying about what may happen in the future is a waste of precious time and robs us of the ability to love life. Worry cannot add a single day to our lives, but it can assuredly take some away.

Perhaps that's why Jesus said, "Don't worry about tomorrow, for tomorrow will bring its own worries. Today's trouble is enough for today" (Matt. 6:34). In this verse, we are given the answer for how to not let life steal our joy: don't stress over the future. *We* don't know what will happen tomorrow, but God does, and He has it all under control.

The first step to overcoming worry and breaking free of stressing about the future is to turn over our problems to God in prayer. Prayer doesn't immediately solve our problems, but it does invite God's peace to fill our hearts. Through prayer we can choose to let Him shoulder our burdens instead of doing it ourselves. When God's peace nestles into our hearts, minds, and spirits, suddenly our problems seem less overwhelming, and we may even think of them less often. The less we think about them, the less we worry.

The second thing we can do is ask God to help us get our thoughts in line with His Word so we can trust Him with all things. Isaiah 26:3 promises, "You will keep him in perfect peace, whose mind is stayed on You, because he trusts in You" (NKJV). If we want peace in our hearts no matter what storms are raging around us, our hearts and minds have to be aligned with God's promises. What we think is how we live.

The third step to overcoming worry is to humbly admit we can't do this thing called life in our own strength and ask God to give us the strength to carry on. Isaiah 40:29–31 promises, "He gives power to the weak and strength to the powerless.... But those who trust in the LORD will find new strength. They will soar high on wings like eagles. They will run and not grow weary. They will walk and not faint."

Perhaps the best antidote to stressing over the future is the belief that God can be trusted to meet all our future needs, just as He did for Ruth and Naomi.

GOD CAN BE TRUSTED

As I look back over the first couple years of being a single mom, I stand in awe of how God gave me the strength to persevere through so many hard days. But I'm most amazed by how He provided for my children and me in ways I could never have imagined.

He provided for our basic needs with money that had been sitting untouched in savings for years, completely unaware that one day it would be what helped us survive. Unexpected checks appeared from time to time in the mailbox and always at just the right time. A family member offered generous gifts to help. Opportunities to earn extra income often fell into my lap. The mortgage company approved a repayment plan which I was told wouldn't get approved in a million years for various reasons, but this allowed my children and me to continue having a roof over our heads. Countless financial situations regarding debts and financial obligations miraculously worked out which didn't make any logical sense at all.

I had been out of the corporate workforce for twelve years, instead working in ministry and staying at home to raise my children. Now as a single parent and provider, I desperately needed a steady income, but I struggled with concerns and insecurities over whether I would ever get hired. Anywhere. Despite having a resume of credentials prior to leaving the corporate world and being fully qualified for the many jobs I applied for, every door seemed to stay closed. So after months of unsuccessfully looking for employment, discouragement had begun to set in, tangled with a hint of panic until God opened the perfect door He had planned for me to walk through. You see, I received an incredible job offer from a ministry I was passionate about. I had worried that in order to survive, I would be forced to take a job in a secular organization or business, which would limit my time for ministry and maybe even result in quitting ministry altogether. But with this new job, not only could I continue my speaking and writing, but I could also serve God's kingdom in new and exciting ways.

But here's the part where God really showed off: I received the call with the job offer on my birthday. An amazing birthday gift from Jesus!

Coincidence? Absolutely not. God-incidence? Absolutely! Just as He did for Naomi and Ruth and my friend Sherri, perfectly orchestrating their lives down to a season or specific day on the calendar, and just as He does for every one of His children, God had been working and putting His miraculous plans for provision into place years and years before they would ever come to fruition. Down to an exact date of His choosing—the exact day I was born and a day when I desperately needed some good news and a reason to celebrate.

I could go on and on with countless examples of how God provided for my family's physical, financial, and emotional needs in ways I never could have expected or planned—much less explained. Time and time again, He provided perfect protection and provision, not a minute late or a minute early. It was all nothing short of miraculous. In fact, after months of seeing God provide for us and protect our family in incredibly supernatural ways, I exclaimed to my children, "I cannot wait to see how God is going to provide for us next month!" I began to finally understand what trusting God and fully depending on Him really looks like. I was able to live each day with peace, joy, and much less stress, because I believed without a shadow of a doubt that God was working things out for our good in the invisible realms. I'm not saying I never worried again about anything (that would be a lie!), but I am saying that when we stop doubting if God is going to protect and provide as His Word promises, life can feel less hectic and happier.

I became intentional about trying to maintain this attitude of expectant faith, which became a determining factor in my ability to stress less about the present and future and to trust God with all of it. My faith and attitude drastically changed simply because I began expectantly and excitedly waiting to see *how* God would protect and provide, not *if* He would.

Before I could learn to love my life again, I had to determine to let go of worry and begin to rest in God's promises of protection and provision in every form. I had to stop obsessing over all the "what-ifs" and believe God would always protect and provide for me. I had to continually seek His strength to stand firm on the hardest of days rather than let my emotions morph into worries and crush my hope and joy. I had to choose to believe in His promises of restoration, in His timing, and in His ways. Day by day I had to choose to trust that God was not only present in my life but also actively orchestrating His plans for meeting my needs, both current and future.

Of course, I still face problems and challenges in my life. But by intentionally choosing to let God worry about tomorrow and believing He has it all figured out, I am able to stay free of the enslavement of constantly stressing and obsessing about what each tomorrow will hold. I can now focus on enjoying and embracing each day I am given the opportunity to live. You can do the same.

Are you living under the weight of worry? Are you carrying stress and anxiety about the future? Is worry stealing your peace, hope, happiness, and maybe even your health? Friend, pray and give your burdens and worries to Him. Let Him carry them for you so you can be free to live life to the fullest with a heart of joy. Get up tomorrow morning with a smile on your face instead of worry in your heart by putting your full trust in God. Remind yourself every morning that He has everything under control, no matter how out of control things feel and appear. And seek God's strength while always remembering that when you feel your weakest, He is at His strongest (see 2 Cor. 12:10).

Let God help you start loving your life again today.

Stay focused on today and let Jesus handle tomorrow.

LOVE YOUR LIFE CHALLENGE #10

Trust that God has your tomorrows taken care of.

Reflect

How often do you stress about the unknowns of the future and allow worry to steal your peace and joy? If it's often, how would trusting in God's protection and provision allow you to embrace the opportunity to enjoy life and live it to the fullest, despite your circumstances?

Is it possible stress and worry could be to blame for some of the health challenges you've recently dealt with? How might reducing your stress through faith help you feel better overall?

Act

Think of the top three things that tend to weigh on your heart regarding the unknowns of the future. Each day, do the following three things for each worrisome unknown:

1. Surrender that worry to God. Tell Him you're letting go of it and giving it to Him, and then try not to think about it again. If it creeps back into your consciousness, immediately surrender it again to God.

2. Do something to get your mind off the worry. Listen to your favorite song, think of a blessing you can praise God for, or do something you enjoy.

3. Ask God to give you patience with yourself and with Him as He transforms your mind and helps you learn to replace worry with full trust and dependence on Him.

Pray

Jesus, forgive me for doubting that You have a good plan in store for me. I seek Your strength and peace to help me let go of my fears and worries about the future, stop obsessing over how things may turn out, and trust that You are holding my future in Your hands. In Your heavenly name, amen.

Smile

Create a bucket list. Think about how you can begin taking steps to reach the goals or realize the dreams in your heart. Let your mind envision living out those goals and dreams, and let those happy thoughts motivate you to work toward achieving them.

11

Develop a Thankful Heart

I stood in the middle of their home and looked around. The floor was nothing more than dirt. No linoleum. No hardwoods. No shiny tiles. No carpets. Just dirt. Furniture was sparse, and the few pieces I saw were shabby and falling apart. The entire family of ten lived in a small, four-quadrant dwelling made of concrete blocks, with plastic tarps for windows and a makeshift ceiling. Family members slept either on the floor or in two small "beds" that consisted of thin blankets draped over a few wooden slats on a rickety bedframe. No mattresses. A single light bulb dangled from the ceiling, the only source of light for the entire home, making it dark and dim within.

The family cooked every meal in their tiny kitchen, not on a stove but over a small fire pit that was nothing more than a hole dug in the dirt floor of the house and filled with small logs and sticks. The day I was there, they were cooking a few handmade tortillas for me and the group I was with. Thick black smoke from the cooking fire filled the room, causing my eyes to burn and water.

The skin on the bottom of all the children's feet, even those of the tiny three-year-old girl, looked like leather, an obvious sign that they had never worn shoes. Their sunburned faces, dirty noses, and torn clothing told a story of a lifetime of poverty, hunger, and desperation. The family had no means of transportation except a donkey. No closets full of clothes. No toys. No kitchen cabinets and refrigerator stocked with food. No phones. No television.

But not once did anyone complain.

I was visiting this family as part of a trip with a child sponsorship organization in Quito, Ecuador. The mother had been anticipating our visit and was excited to show us her home. This sweet woman beamed from ear to ear as she taught us how to pull corn from the stalks, grind grain, and knead dough into flat, round pancakes that we cooked over the smoky fire. She couldn't speak English but explained through our interpreter that her husband had deserted her, leaving her to care for their children all alone. Her brother had stepped up to help, but he had tragically died. She said she was doing the best she could under the circumstances.

But, oh, how her eyes sparkled. Despite all the things this woman lacked (at least in our Western eyes), her heart lacked nothing. She was filled with the joy of Christ. She loved her life because she chose to love the life God had given her. Instead of feeling embarrassed and making excuses for what she didn't have or feeling sorry for herself, she boasted about all God had done for them.

Not once did I see her lose her beaming smile. Not once did I see any of the children whining or fighting with one another, but instead, they tenderly cared for one another. Not once did I hear her young daughter, probably nine years old, complain about her back hurting after carrying a baby in a sack for hours during our visit.

This family smiled, laughed, and thanked God for their blessings. Their attitudes showed optimism in the face of negative circumstances and extreme poverty. And their mouths praised the Lord.

Throughout the remainder of that week, as I visited the homes of several families in similar situations, my heart began to ache, not only for these sweet people who were happy with so little but also because of the sad state of ungratefulness in my own heart. After being with these people, I realized I needed a major attitude adjustment. I suddenly felt ashamed that despite the enormity of the blessings I had been given, I discounted them because I was too busy counting my problems or the things I thought I needed or deserved.

While this heart-changing, eye-opening adventure happened over ten years ago, I still remember boarding the flight to head home and asking God to help me remember the families I had met and their amazing attitudes of gratitude. I never wanted to forget their deep gratefulness for every tiny blessing that had been bestowed on them. They had learned to have thankful hearts by focusing on the Giver of the gifts instead of the gifts themselves.

Being thankful for the good things God has given us is really just being glad we are benefiting from those good things and are able to enjoy them. But being truly thankful requires looking beyond our blessings to the Holy One who blesses. It's about being full of gratitude for Christ Himself, instead of simply appreciating the gifts He has given us.

MAKE TIME FOR THANKFULNESS

Luke 17:11–19 tells a story about a group of men who all received an immense blessing, but only one had a heart full of thanks to the Giver of that blessing. In this passage, Jesus was on His way to Jerusalem when He came to the entrance of a village. Off in the distance were ten men with leprosy. Upon recognizing Jesus, they began to shout and beg for merciful healing. Jesus told them to go to the priests, and they did as He instructed. Miraculously, all ten lepers were healed of this terrible disease.

Ten men healed. Ten men immensely blessed by the love of Jesus. But only one had a thankful heart.

"One of them, when he saw that he was healed, came back to Jesus, shouting, 'Praise God!' He fell to the ground at Jesus' feet, thanking him for what he had done. This man was a Samaritan" (vv. 15–16). I can't help but envision a smile sweeping across Jesus' face as He stood in front of this man who was so grateful for the gift he had received. But that smile may have quickly faded when Jesus realized that none of the others had returned to express gratefulness.

In verses 17–19, we read of His disappointment: "Jesus asked, 'Didn't I heal ten men? Where are the other nine? Has no one returned to give glory to God except this foreigner?' And Jesus said to the man, 'Stand up and go. Your faith has healed you.'" This former leper was so filled with gratitude for his blessing of healing that he threw himself at the feet of Jesus and worshipped Him. This man's obedience healed his body, but his gratitude healed his soul.

I wish I could identify with the one leper who ran back to Jesus, but too often my response is much like that of the nine who didn't. Maybe yours is too. Ungratefulness is a serious obstacle when it comes to loving the life we are given. A lack of gratitude will always morph into a lack of joy.

I wonder, why didn't the others return? Maybe one or more of them thought their healing was just coincidence or some other miraculous form of healing but not from Jesus. Maybe they thought they deserved to be healed and didn't see the need to thank Him. Maybe they wanted to be healed but didn't want to live up to the expectations of being a follower of Jesus, therefore they shied away from going back and being confronted with that possibility. Maybe they were so busy telling their families and friends of their healing that they simply forgot to thank the One who had healed them. Maybe they ran off and started doing things they'd always wanted to do. Maybe after all the years of being outcasts, they wanted to get on with their lives and didn't have any spare time to go back and thank Jesus. Maybe they just didn't see the need or didn't even think about it.

We don't know the reasons these men didn't express their gratitude to the One who had blessed and healed them, but that's not the point of this story. Here's the takeaway: this passage helps us recognize the importance of fostering a thankful heart, no matter what anyone else does. And how do we do that? By focusing on the Giver of our blessings and not just on the blessings themselves.

COUNT YOUR BLESSINGS, NOT YOUR PROBLEMS

Max Lucado tells this story about a friend who learned the secret to having a thankful heart:

> My friend Jerry has taught me the value of gratitude. He is seventy-eight years old and regularly shoots his age on the golf course. (If I ever do the same, I'll need to live to be a hundred.) His dear wife, Ginger, battles Parkinson's disease. What should have been a wonderful season of retirement has been marred by multiple hospital stays, medication, and struggles. Many days she cannot keep her balance. Jerry has to be at her side. Yet he never complains. He always has a smile and a joke. And he relentlessly beats me in golf. I asked Jerry his secret. He said, "Every morning Ginger

and I sit together and sing a hymn. I ask her what she wants to sing. She always says, 'Count Your Blessings.' So we sing it. And we count our blessings."[1]

Growing up, I loved that hymn and must have sung it in church hundreds of times. But the meaning of its words did not fully sink into my heart until I got older and realized the value of actually doing what this hymn says.

> When upon life's billows you are tempest tossed,
> When you are discouraged, thinking all is lost,
> Count your many blessings,
> name them one by one,
> And it will surprise you what
> the Lord hath done.[2]

When we make it a practice to count our blessings instead of our problems, the way we look at life will change. We'll gradually form a habit of living a thankful life, because when our hearts are full of gratitude to God, our lives will feel full too.

If we are counting our blessings, we won't have time to count all our problems. If we are counting our blessings, we will realize all is not lost and happiness can be ours. If we are counting our blessings, we'll recognize we truly do have much to be thankful for, despite our hardships. Our doubts about God's goodness and favor will fly away, and we will have a new perspective on our lives.

We might even be surprised at the number of blessings we inadvertently overlooked, simply because we never stopped long enough to actually count them and thank Jesus for them.

When was the last time you counted your blessings?

As believers, we have many blessings to be grateful for, and at the top of our lists should be all the things we have in Christ.

Despite what we feel our lives are lacking and the problems we are facing, we always have the choice to worship the Giver of every blessing. We can always live thankful for what we have in Christ and for the gift of life. Life in and of itself—every breath we take—is a blessing.

BEING THANKFUL WHEN YOU DON'T FEEL LIKE IT

When life is going smoothly, thankfulness is rather easy. But when our lives are in a downward spiral, or when one wave of problems crashes in after another, having a thankful heart starts feeling a lot less natural.

Out of curiosity I recently pulled up my digital journal on my computer and did a word search for *thankful*. I wanted to see how many times, if at all, I had written words of thankfulness in the first two years after my husband left. I was pleasantly surprised, and my spirits were lifted, as I scrolled through the dozens of pages where *thankful* popped up in yellow on the screen. But it wasn't just the many mentions of thankfulness that made my heart leap; it was also the pattern I noticed of what I was expressing thankfulness for.

You know what I thanked God for over and over again in the aftermath of life getting turned upside down? Not cars, clothes, food, vacations, or any type of material item. Not successes, accomplishments, or opportunities. Not problem-free days or sufficient spending money in my checking account. My gratitude was for people—precious friends, beloved family, my children. Encouraging text messages received just when I needed them. Perfectly timed Scripture verses and devotional readings. Gardenias brought in from the backyard, filling the house with sweet fragrance. Sunshine. The smell of rain. The beach. The soothing sound of the waves on the beach. Christmas music. A messy house, signifying my home was full of people and conversation. My faith. My Jesus.

These were the things that mattered most during a season when it seemed unlikely that I could feel gratitude. Each of these precious gifts I was most grateful for helped me keep my focus on God and not on my circumstances. They drew me closer to Him as they helped me develop a thankful heart. During this time when I was juggling more challenges than I could handle, I became grateful for completely different things than I had been in the past. My gratitude changed from being gift-centered gratitude to God-centered gratitude.

God used this difficult season to groom my heart to focus on Him instead of on the tangible blessings my gratitude used to focus on. He slowly changed my mind-set, and over time all the things that once seemed so important and necessary paled in comparison with the gifts I was enjoying now. I finally understood what it meant to be thankful for the gift of life and for the Giver from whom all blessings flow. You see, I learned to be grateful simply for God, for who He is and His presence and activity in my life. Not just for the blessings I could see and touch.

If you want to foster a more thankful heart, ask God to help you become aware of and grateful for the things you often take for granted. As you learn to thank Him for situations and circumstances you don't enjoy and to trust He will somehow bring good out of them, He will transform your heart and mind. You will begin to see that often it is the simplest of blessings that we should be most thankful for.

START LIVING THE THANKFUL LIFE

Today is a great day to start living with a thankful heart, to begin counting your blessings one by one and being grateful for the Giver of those blessings. I encourage you to do two things at least once a day.

First, thank God for who He is. If it seems His presence is far away and you can't see Him at work or hear His voice, ask Him for the ability to see and hear Him more. If you ask, you will receive. Remember, if you feel far from God, it is not He who has moved. He's still there with open arms. Move in closer to Him.

Second, ask yourself, what blessings from God are you enjoying today? Think about what you see, hear, smell, and touch; consider the people in your life; consider your material possessions and the ways God has provided for you and protected you. Think about the things that give you joy and bring your life meaning. All these are good gifts from the Lord. Thank Him for these gifts.

When our hearts are full of thanks for the blessings we can see with our hearts as well as with our eyes, we can't help but feel joy for the lives we are living.

LOVE YOUR LIFE CHALLENGE #11

Practice a life of gratitude.

Reflect

Is your gratitude typically focused on the gifts or the Giver of the gifts? What changes might you need to make in order to start living with a more thankful heart?

Have you spent more time lately counting your problems or counting your blessings?

Act

Go outside and look for a small, smooth rock you can carry in your pocket or purse everywhere you go. Each time your hand touches the rock, let it serve as a reminder to thank God for at least one thing in your life. And each time, express thanks for the Giver of your blessings as well.

Pray

Lord, forgive me for being ungrateful for all You have given me and done for me or, at a minimum, neglecting to live with a heart full of thanks. I commit to being thankful for You and who You are, not only for what I think You are blessing me with. In Jesus' name, amen.

Smile

Buy a beautiful journal and make it your gratitude journal. Record everything you are thankful for: the smell of clean laundry, a child's laugh, a hug from a loved one, tangible blessings, the blessing of friendships, a special way God provided for you, etc. The next time you're feeling down, pull out your gratitude journal and let it remind you to smile. And while it's open, record something new you are grateful for.

12

Be the Answer to Someone's Prayer

It was a record-setting day in July in the South, with the temperature reaching three digits, when I received her panicked phone call. My daughter had left her after-school cheerleading-practice outfit at home—again. I begrudgingly jumped in the hot car to head toward her school and immediately began grumbling about the heat and the perspiration already dripping from my brow.

A few miles down the road, with the air-conditioning blowing full blast on my face, a divine encounter interrupted my frustration. I suddenly noticed a frail and pregnant woman up ahead, walking at the edge of the busy highway. She was wearing a bulky long-sleeved shirt and pants that hung from her tiny body and very pregnant belly—clearly inappropriate attire for such a blistering day, not to mention the fact that the clothes were obviously men's. She was walking slowly with her head down, exhaustion and despair evident in her posture. I passed by her at sixty miles an hour. While my initial response was to keep on driving, my heart just wouldn't listen.

I looked in the rearview mirror to catch another glimpse. Sadness filled my spirit, and I had a strong sense of God nudging me to help this total stranger. But as my hands gripped the hot steering wheel, excuses gripped my mind. *I'm already late and cheer practice is about to start. My daughter will be penalized for forgetting her clothes again. I'm in a huge hurry, God. It's dangerous to pick up strangers on the side of the road, right? I mean, who does that? Other people might think I'm crazy if I stop to help. Surely someone else will help her.*

As the cool air from the vents blew my hair across my face, God's voice whispered to my spirit, reminding me of Matthew 25:40, which talks about helping the "least of these." God's pull to turn around and help this woman became stronger than my urge to keep driving and ignore her. So I disregarded all the excuses in my head, slowed down, did a U-turn, and headed back in the opposite direction of where I needed to go.

Fortunately, there were no cars behind me as I slowed down and pulled up beside her. She stopped and looked at me with a hint of fear. I rolled down the window, smiled, and asked if she needed help. Her hollow eyes were full of surprise, I assume because a stranger was offering to come to her aid. She told me she was a couple of hours from home and had been delivering phone books in the area. She'd been headed home so she could feed her six children, who were waiting for her to return, when her car had run out of gas. That was bad enough, but to make matters worse, she had no money to purchase a fuel container, much less any gas. When I asked her how

far along she was in her pregnancy, she said eight and a half months.
I knew even if she'd made it to a gas station and been able to purchase
some gas, she never could have carried a heavy container with several
gallons of gas all the way back to her stalled vehicle. She looked as if
she didn't have the strength to take another step.

The nearest gas station was five miles away—way too far for any
woman, especially a very pregnant one, to be walking in blistering
temperatures. Her situation was hopeless and heartbreaking. She was
helpless and afraid, thirsty and needy. She'd been aimlessly walking
down the road because she didn't have a clue what else to do. It was
evident she and her unborn child were in danger and I was her only
hope.

In that moment, this helpless woman was indeed the "least of
these" Jesus mentioned in Matthew 25:37–40: "Then these righteous
ones will reply, 'Lord, when did we ever see you hungry and feed
you? Or thirsty and give you something to drink? Or a stranger and
show you hospitality? Or naked and give you clothing? When did we
ever see you sick or in prison and visit you?' And the King will say,
'I tell you the truth, when you did it to one of the least of these my
brothers and sisters, you were doing it to me!'"

In this passage Jesus was teaching the importance of caring for
those the world has dismissed or overlooked. In these verses He was
saying when we are compassionate and offer help to the marginalized
in society, we are also caring for Him. Our loving actions on behalf
of the "least of these" are equivalent to serving the Savior and loving
Him. The faithful ones who show compassion and tangible love for
others are the ones to inherit His kingdom (see v. 46).

Compassion gripped my heart. I pushed aside my to-do list and my excuses so I could help one person in need. One of God's girls. I admit, I was taking a bit of a risk—this woman could have been someone different from who she appeared to be. But I had to trust the Holy Spirit's prompting to help her, so I told her I would help her with whatever she needed in order to get home safely.

When I arrived late at my daughter's practice with a disheveled pregnant woman in the passenger seat of my car (because I had to deliver the practice clothes before going to the gas station and the stalled vehicle!), trust me, some people thought I was a little crazy. Especially my daughter. I knew I would have to explain to her later why I had taken the risk of picking up a stranger from the side of the road, but in that moment, nothing could have stolen the joy from my heart. What a privilege it was that God had blessed me with the opportunity to be the answer to someone else's prayers!

But here's the thing: I don't think God nudged my heart to help this woman just so she could benefit from my assistance. I believe He also wanted to force me to pause, open my eyes, and be aware that I needed to take my focus off myself, my busyness, and my own issues long enough to remember that putting others' needs before our own is a blessing in and of itself. When we exhibit sacrificial empathy and compassion, God's light shines through us. When we put aside our own plans and pay attention to those people He has placed on our hearts—instead of viewing them as interruptions—we extend to others the grace and mercy Jesus extended to us.

When I drove this precious woman back to her car and put several gallons of gas into the fuel tank, she meekly waved at me with a big smile, something I hadn't seen until that moment, and she quietly uttered the words, "God bless you."

In my heart I knew He already had.

BE A BLESSING, REAP A BLESSING

I promise you this: when we give of ourselves to others, we are the ones who receive the most.

You may be wondering, *But how am I supposed to find someone to help?* By praying and asking God to help you see through love-colored glasses so your eyes will see what He sees and your heart will break for what breaks His. People in need are all around us everywhere we go. However, their need may not be as glaringly obvious as it was with this frail pregnant woman walking down a busy highway in three-digit heat, dressed in men's winter clothing. But when we ask God for open hearts and open eyes, He will grant that request. He will show us the people around us who need us to be the hands and feet of Jesus and will prick our hearts to help.

In this broken world, many people are in need of help. Help might take the form of spending time with someone who is stuck at home because of an illness. Help might be an offer to an exhausted mother to babysit her children for free so she can have a break. Help might take the form of volunteering at a local school, church, charity, or ministry.

When we intentionally learn to look through the lens of love, keeping God's instructions about caring for the "least of these" in our minds, we free up our hearts to see not only the needs of others but also creative ways to help meet them. The more we step out to serve, the more we see people's needs and understand how trivial our excuses are for not helping meet those needs. When we give our time, hearts, and love to others in any way, we feel a sense of joy, accomplishment, and fulfillment.

Giving of our time and resources to help those in need doesn't only make the world better—it makes our lives better too. The truth is, being the hands and feet of Jesus enables us to love life more, feel better about ourselves, and live happier lives in general. Even if our circumstances don't change and problems remain, our outlook on life will be different if we have helped meet the needs of another soul. To have genuinely loved someone, just as Jesus did and as He calls us to do, is a blessing you don't want to miss. Being a blessing is a blessing. When you love your life, you can love with your life.

A KEY TO HAPPINESS

In 2015 the *Huffington Post* published an article called "10 Facts That Prove Helping Others Is a Key to Achieving Happiness." According to the article, studies show that the act of giving back or helping others has an emotional impact on us. When you help someone in need or do any kind of charitable act, "the portion of the brain responsible for feelings of reward [is] triggered. The brain also releases feel-good chemicals and spurs you to perform more kind acts—something psychologists call 'helper's high.'"[1] The article also referred to research that shows people who help others have stronger friendships and better overall well-being.

In a similar vein, Mark Snyder, the director of the University of Minnesota's Center for the Study of the Individual and Society, said, "People who volunteer tend to have higher self-esteem, psychological well-being, and happiness.... All of these things ... [improve] their health and even their longevity."[2]

Joy is found when we stop making life all about us and start making it about other people instead. Romans 7:4 says, "And now you are united with the one who was raised from the dead. As a result, we can produce a harvest of good deeds for God." When we act on the God-given desire to serve others, we feel blessed and happy. Jesus encouraged us to help others in big and small ways because He knows we benefit from loving others as much as those who are receiving our love.

When we have a heart for Jesus, we can't help but have a heart for others. When we pray for God to give us an acute awareness of other people's needs, our own needs begin to seem less important. When we are more concerned with helping others with their problems than constantly grumbling or worrying about our own, our burdens feel a little less heavy. When we serve other people and pour our lives into theirs, it lifts not only their hearts but our hearts too. Jesus commands us to care for the "least of these" because doing so leads to living abundantly.

Proverbs 11:25 says, "The generous will prosper; those who refresh others will themselves be refreshed." *The Message* puts it this way: "The one who blesses others is abundantly blessed; those who help others are helped." I love how Charles Spurgeon described the meaning of these verses:

> The general principle is, that in living for the good of others, we shall be profited also ourselves. We must not isolate our own interests but feel that we live for others.... God has so constituted this universe, that selfishness is the greatest possible offence against his law, and living for others, and ministering to others, is the strictest obedience to his will. Our surest road to our own happiness is to seek the good of our fellows. We store up in God's own bank what we generously expend on the behalf of our race.[3]

Simply put, the road to happiness is paved through the helping and building up of others.

Jesus devoted His life to helping others. Although Jesus did make time for self-care, He constantly put the needs of others before His own, whether those of a beggar, a prostitute, a Samaritan, a widow, a prisoner, someone riddled with disease, someone nailing His hands and feet to a piece of wood, or even someone who had recently died. When people interrupted Him while He was busy, He viewed it as an opportunity to serve them. Such compassion doesn't come naturally to us, but faith is the fuel that inspires us to be selfless.

When in faith we ask God to open our hearts and show us how to be the hands and feet of Jesus to others, He will answer that prayer. When our eyes are open, we'll begin to see needs we were previously blind to. We'll notice that an elderly neighbor's yard needs to be mowed, we'll feel compelled to take dinner to someone who just got home from the hospital, or we'll offer to sit at the bedside of someone in hospice to give the family respite. No matter whether the need we meet is big or small, oh, what a blessing it is to be used by the Creator of the universe to show the people He created that they matter.

Helping others is a privilege, not just a responsibility, and with privilege comes great joy.

LOVE YOUR LIFE CHALLENGE #12

Do something nice for someone else every day.

Reflect

Have you been so consumed with your own life, challenges, and responsibilities you've neglected to see the people God wants you to see?

How can you be the hands and feet of Jesus this week, even if just for five minutes?

Act

Think of at least one kind thing you can do for someone today. Then actually do it.

Pray

God, I long for a heart that strives to serve the "least of these," and I want to be Your hands and feet in this broken and hurting world. Open doors of opportunity where You want me to serve, and allow me the blessing of being a blessing to another one of Your children. In Jesus' name, amen.

Smile

Put aside all your excuses and do some type of exercise today. Exercise has a profound effect on our happiness and overall well-being. It may feel hard, but afterward you will smile.

Reignite Your Faith

I once heard a story about an incredible sermon that changed a man's life, yet the pastor who gave the sermon never uttered a word.

A man who had been attending a particular church suddenly stopped going to services. After several weeks of noticing the man was not there, the pastor decided to pay him a visit. He put on his coat to keep warm in the freezing-cold winter air and set out toward the man's house. Upon arriving, the pastor knocked on the door, and the man welcomed him in. Knowing why the pastor had come to visit him, the man felt a little embarrassed and wasn't quite sure what to say. So he gestured for the pastor to take a seat in front of the blazing fire. The two men sat down and stared at the dancing flames.

After a few minutes of awkward silence, the pastor bent down, picked up the fire tongs, and poked at the burning logs. A small ember fell off into the ashes, and he used the tongs to pick it up. But instead of placing the ember back in the fire, he placed it off to the side of the hearth, away from the flames. Then he sat back in his chair, leaving the man to wonder what he was doing.

The ember's flame began to diminish until it died completely. Its glow was gone, and within minutes it had grown cold. The pastor then leaned in, picked up the cold ember with the tongs, and placed it back in the flames. Immediately the ember began to glow again.

The pastor then rose to leave and thanked the man for allowing him in.

The man smiled and shook the pastor's hand. Then he said, "Thank you so much for your visit and especially for the fiery sermon. I shall be back in church next Sunday."[1]

The point of this story is that if we want our faith to keep burning in our hearts, we must be part of a church family and engage in weekly worship. The fellowship of other believers fans the flame of our faith and helps it thrive. Equally important is that we fan the flame of our faith through a vital relationship with God every day.

This chapter about the importance of having passionate faith and an intimate relationship with God was saved for last not because it is the least important but because it is the most important. If you don't remember anything else you've read thus far, please remember this: if you truly want to love your life again, you have to love Jesus first.

Romans 12:11 says, "Don't burn out; keep yourselves fueled and aflame" (THE MESSAGE). Much like an ember taken from the flames, our faith will grow cold if we don't make it a priority. When our faith becomes lifeless and routine, our joy and love for life begin to flicker and can even disappear. When faith is lacking, joy too will decrease.

So how can you light a fire in your heart for Christ? The answer is simple but takes time and dedication, just like the fostering and maintaining of any relationship. To keep your faith alive, you must stay in touch with Jesus, through conversation with Him and through His Word, and you must stay in community with other believers who will motivate and encourage you to grow and mature in your faith.

During those times when you begin to feel as if the embers of your faith are growing cold, when your heart feels empty and it seems as if something is missing from life, or when joy appears to be a thing of the past, it is time to take action. Here are three things you can do to reignite your faith and keep its fire burning brightly.

1. ADMIT YOU FEEL DISTANT FROM GOD

"Restore to me the joy of your salvation" (Ps. 51:12).

Invite God to reignite the fire in your heart, just as He did in Luke 24 for some followers of Jesus. Three days after Jesus' crucifixion, two of His followers were walking down a road, mourning His death and talking about all that had happened, including the mystery of His missing body. Jesus appeared and began walking beside them, but they didn't recognize Him because God kept them from doing so (see v. 16). Jesus asked them, "What are you discussing so intently as you walk along?" (v. 17), and they began to tell Him all the events that had led up to the crucifixion and how the body of Jesus was missing.

They said, "We had hoped he was the Messiah who had come to rescue Israel" (v. 21). Clearly they doubted whether Jesus was the Promised One.

> Then Jesus said to them, "You foolish people! You
> find it so hard to believe all that the prophets wrote
> in the Scriptures. Wasn't it clearly predicted that the
> Messiah would have to suffer all these things before
> entering his glory?" Then Jesus took them through
> the writings of Moses and all the prophets, explain-
> ing from all the Scriptures the things concerning
> himself. (vv. 25–27)

Basically, Jesus preached the truths of the Old Testament to them and lit a spark in their hearts, making their "hearts burn" within them (v. 32). Jesus taught them all about Himself, and it changed them.

2. SPEND TIME LEARNING ALL ABOUT GOD BY READING HIS WORD

"It takes more than bread to stay alive. It takes a steady stream of words from God's mouth" (Matt. 4:4 THE MESSAGE).

Believers often talk about having a quiet time with God, but not everyone understands what a "quiet time" really is. A quiet time is sitting down with God's Word, just you and Him, and letting Him speak to you through it. In other words, don't simply read the Bible as you would a novel you're trying to finish. Read it with great anticipation of how God will speak to you through it. Read each verse slowly, pondering what each sentence means. If you stumble over something interesting or perplexing, don't just skip over it. Instead, search for the deeper meaning by looking up the passage in a study Bible and reading the commentary. Ask God to illuminate or draw your attention to Scriptures that apply to you in your everyday life.

Having quiet time with God is as simple as removing yourself from the busyness of life, even if for a short period, so you can have intimate time with your heavenly Father. If you want to get to know God, you need to study His Word.

Here are a few ideas for where to start:

- The book of John. If you are a new believer, this book is a great place to start spending intimate time with the Savior. This gospel gives you great insight into who Jesus is and what His ministry was all about.

- Any of the other gospels—Matthew, Mark, or Luke. Commit to reading one or several chapters a day. If something piques your interest, stands out, or appears relevant to a situation you are facing, write it down. It could be something that God wants to say to you.

- The book of Psalms. The psalms are full of encouragement, and this book is a great place to find hope for the trials of life. The psalms help us truly grasp that God is with us and for us at all times.

- The book of Proverbs. Consider reading one chapter a day, jotting down each nugget of wisdom or biblical instruction for living day-to-day life.

- Join a community or church Bible study that is focusing on a specific book or character in the Bible. Then when that one is done, sign up for another.

- Purchase a chronological Bible. There are various chronological Bibles available. While it includes every word of Scripture, a chronological Bible tells events in the order they actually happened and helps God's story read like an amazing novel. Take notes each day on what you read.

As you study God's Word and learn more about Jesus, your eyes will be opened to the truths of Scripture and how to apply them to your life. His Word will ignite fire for Christ in your heart—just as it did for the men Jesus was walking with in Luke 24. "They said to each other, 'Didn't our hearts burn within us as he talked with us on the road and explained the Scriptures to us?'" (v. 32). These men got to know the Word of God because it was taught to them by *the* Word of God. As Jesus opened the Scriptures to them, He kindled a fire in their hearts. Their sorrow was replaced with unshakable joy and their hearts were set ablaze. They went on to find others to tell about all they had experienced and learned. Because their hearts were on fire, they were equipped to help ignite other hearts for Jesus.

If we don't have a personal relationship with Jesus, our hearts are like that cold ember left on the hearth. The good news is, when we spend time studying Scripture, we scoot in a little closer to Jesus and to the fire that warms us up from the inside out and can keep our hearts ablaze.

3. SPEND TIME IN CONVERSATION WITH JESUS EVERY DAY

"Pray continually" (1 Thess. 5:17 NIV).

Quiet time can also be as simple as a time you pour out your heart to God in prayer, talking with Him like the best friend He is and listening for His whispers. A time you invite Him into the quietness of the moment. It may seem awkward at first, but this holy quiet time with God can become something you look forward to as you become more aware of hearing His voice and as the nudgings of the Holy Spirit increase.

Even if you're stuck in traffic, standing in the shower, lying in your bed, walking through the mall, or sitting on the couch with your little one, Jesus is always close, ready, and listening. He is always ready to sit quietly with you no matter where you are. When we talk, He is there to commune with us. We can keep the conversation going as long as we like. His ears are always open. It's never too late to start practicing the habit I mentioned earlier of never saying amen.

These three habits are the sparks that light a fire in our hearts and keep it burning.

FAN THE FLAME DAILY

I encourage you to start making quiet time a priority. Get on your knees and pray. Admit your weaknesses. Be honest with God about your feelings. Tell Him what you need and what your heart longs for. Praise Him for who He is. Thank Him for what He's done for you and the many blessings He has given you. Seek Him with your whole heart and get back into His Word. Ask Him to fill you with the strength, peace, joy, and hope our broken world is trying to steal from you.

Fan the flame of faith every day. Get involved with other believers and fill your life with worship. Walk as closely with Him as you can, and keep your heart's embers burning. The light from your fire will not only keep you warm but also spread to those around you, lighting a spark of interest in other people's hearts to know the

Savior. A heart on fire for Christ will always lead to a life full of joy and happiness.

It excites me beyond belief to think God has opened your eyes to see what areas of your heart and mind need to change so you can appreciate and enjoy the life He has given you, regardless of all the situations that might be difficult or unfair. I hope you are ready to begin living life to the fullest.

LOVE YOUR LIFE CHALLENGE #13

Reignite the fire for Christ in your heart and keep it aflame.

Reflect

Have you pulled away from church or Christian fellowship for one reason or another? How could getting involved with a community of believers again help you enjoy life more? In what ways could doing so help you become stronger in your faith?

Has the fire in your heart faded because of not consistently and faithfully walking and talking with Jesus? How might reigniting your fire for Christ change your entire life from this point forward, and what step can you take today to light it again?

Act

Don't have a home church? Start looking online for one in your community today and commit to going this Sunday. Haven't been in a Bible study for quite some time—or ever? Look for Bible studies in your community or local church and join one, even if it's already started. Has it been months since you opened your Bible and asked God to speak to you? Take your Bible off the shelf, blow off the dust, and let God breathe fresh life and hope into your heart. Sign up for a daily email devotional, download a morning devotional mobile app, or subscribe to an inspiring Christian podcast. Take at least one step toward rekindling the fire in your heart while asking God to help you stay close to the fire as you embark on a new adventure of faith.

Pray

Dear Jesus, please draw me back to You. I have felt empty but couldn't put my finger on what was wrong. I knew I didn't feel joy or happiness, but I wasn't sure exactly why and blamed it on all the problems in my life or on Your perceived lack of attention to those problems. Forgive me for not trusting You. I am ready to be on fire for You again and live life to the fullest. Ignite my heart today! I am choosing to love my life again, and I praise You for helping me begin to feel joyful, happy, content, and at peace again! In Your most precious name I pray, amen.

Smile

Think about something you are passionate about. Consider how God could use this passion in a way that would glorify Him. Pray for Him to give you clarity and direction regarding the purpose He has for your life. When passion and purpose intersect, life takes on a whole new meaning and joy becomes unshakable. Do something in faith that will make you—and God—smile.

Conclusion

Several times throughout this book I've mentioned John 10:10 because I want its promise to settle deep in your heart: "I have come that they may have life, and have it to the full" (NIV). Jesus wants us to enjoy life abundantly! But this verse also reminds us that we have an enemy who is working against us in the dark, trying to suck the joy out of our hearts and destroy our faith: "The thief comes only to steal and kill and destroy" (NIV).

The Devil doesn't want you to enjoy your life. He wants you to stay discouraged and dissatisfied because he knows that when you are down in the dumps, the embers in your heart will grow a little bit colder for Christ and maybe for life altogether. He wants you to blame God, turn your back on Him, and convince yourself that you can do a better job of running your life than He can.

Don't give the enemy what he wants.

Jesus tells us His purpose is to give you, His child, a rich and satisfying life. He has already won the battle for your heart; now let Him help you be victorious over the enemy's attempts to steal your joy and destroy your love for the life God has given you. *The Message* translates Jesus' promise beautifully: "I came so they can have real and eternal life, more and better life than they ever dreamed of."

Did you hear that? You can have a better life than you ever dreamed of! This holy promise is 100 percent true and can happen for you. But know this—every suggestion in every chapter of this book hinges on your faith, because when you commit to living on fire for Jesus and choose the abundant life He promises, the enemy of our souls takes notice.

This means that when you begin to implement the Love Your Life Challenges at the end of each chapter, your life won't necessarily get easier. In fact, it might even seem harder. With great faith comes great opposition. When we face great opposition, we can be tempted to simply give up because giving up seems easier than continuing to fight the battle for joy. But with great opposition also comes a great God, who is more powerful than the one who wants us to stay joyless and hopeless.

DON'T GIVE UP; GOD UP

So don't give up; God up instead. Ever heard the phrase *Man up*? It essentially just means to be brave and courageous or to tough it out when an unpleasant situation pops up. It means don't quit or give up but instead keep pushing through in your own strength and willpower. The phrase *God up* means to do exactly the same thing, except in the power of Jesus Christ. Trying to man up— or woman up—and do life in our own power will always lead to discouragement, exhaustion, and burnout. But as I've already said, when we are weak, He is strong (see 2 Cor. 12:10).

Be ready for a fight to the finish. You and your heart are worth it, and your God is standing tall and mighty as your defender.

Be mindful that there will be days when you will want to throw up your hands and yell, "I can't take this anymore!" Days when you will want to crawl under the covers and hide from the world or will secretly wish you could start living someone else's life, someone whose life seems easier to love than your own. Days when you're tired of putting on a mask. Days when trying to keep a smile in your heart and on your face seems like an impossible task. Days when it feels as if you can't find a single reason to be joyful and can't muster up the strength to even try.

There will be days when you will be tempted to give up on God and give in to a life of discouragement, hopelessness, and joylessness. It's even possible that this is where you find yourself today (or how you found yourself feeling before you picked up a book talking about learning to love your life again!). If so, please stop right now and choose to look *up* to God instead of *around* at your problems. Those moments when you feel like giving up are the exact moments when you need to God up with all the strength you have in Him.

All things are possible when Christ is at the center of our lives. Even when we feel like giving up, He can give us the strength to carry on. He can give us the power to purposely and passionately love the lives we have and live the abundant lives Jesus intended for us. Just ask the apostle Paul.

In 2 Corinthians 4, Paul encouraged the church of Corinth not to give up, especially when it came to defending the gospel. He reminded the people that they all held a treasure in their hearts—the light of the gospel—which was the sole reason they could keep persevering when they felt like quitting in the face of adversities. Verse 1 says, "Therefore, since God in his mercy has given us this new way, we never give up." Although he stumbled in his faith at times, Paul consistently kept his eyes focused on God. The "new way" he was referring to in this verse has to do with the fact that because of the Holy Spirit living within us, we can freely enjoy the divine gifts of peace, grace, mercy, hope, joy, and strength. We no longer have to follow the rules and regulations in the Old Testament in order to try to earn God's favor. Throughout Scripture we read over and over that every time Paul wanted to give up, he chose to God up instead. He routinely chose to depend on God's power and strength instead of his own.

Paul experienced more suffering than any one person should have to endure, and likely more than we ever will. Over his lifetime, Paul was imprisoned, beaten, stoned, shipwrecked, and chased mercilessly by enemies. He suffered mental and spiritual exhaustion in addition to physical pain, hunger, thirst, and at times even a lack of clothing. If you ask me, that's enough to make anyone want to give up! Yet he never did. His faith and trust in Jesus as his Savior equipped and inspired him to keep from giving up, even when he had every earthly reason to do so.

As Paul made the choice to God up instead of give up, God filled him with strength and perseverance he never could have found on his own. He purposely lived life to the fullest because of Whose he was. He knew God had given him only one life to live, and he was determined to make the most of it. Paul wanted to use his life to glorify his Savior, no matter what it took. He could have spent his life being angry about all his hardships, suffering, and disappointments. But he chose to be thankful for the life he had. He trusted that God was always with him and had a good purpose and plan for everything He allowed Paul to endure. Paul chose to love life, love God, and live with joy and peace and a thankful heart, time and time again.

And so can you.

Max Lucado wrote, "What you have in Christ is greater than anything you don't have in life. You have God, who is crazy about you, and the forces of heaven to monitor and protect you. You have the living presence of Jesus within you. In Christ you have everything."[1] Remember this truth the next time you feel like giving up in your quest to love your life. Take a deep breath and adjust your vision. Look at what God has done in your life, rather than what you feel He has not done yet. Commit to trusting Him, instead of doubting His ways. Surrender your burdens and stop trying to fix everything on your own or wishing you could. Refocus on trusting the only One who actually can fix everything that is broken.

LIFE IS PRECIOUS

There are always going to be circumstances in life that make us unhappy. Sadness and grief are unavoidable. People will break our hearts. Disappointments will discourage us. Dreams will die, and relationships will end. Life can indeed be hard, making it seem as if it is impossible to ever feel joy again. But it's not.

Through the strength and power you have in Christ, you can choose to be happy and live with joy, no matter what life throws at you. You can choose to take a leap of faith and trust that God's promise of abundant life is within your reach and meant for you.

Every one of God's children is meant to live an extraordinary life, rich in abundant blessings. Wherever you find yourself and however you are feeling, will you commit to living today to the fullest? Don't let another day slip away without feeling the joy God wants you to have. Life is precious, and time is limited. So why waste another day just existing instead of truly living?

Bronnie Ware is a former nurse who spent several years caring for terminally ill patients who were in the last few weeks on earth. She recorded the regrets people talked about as they were nearing the end of their lives and eventually turned that record into an article and then a book called *The Top Five Regrets of the Dying*. More than three million people read the article the first year it was released.[2]

When Bronnie looked at all the regrets people shared with her, she was able to identify five that her dying patients mentioned again and again in one way or another.

1. I wish I'd had the courage to live a life true to myself, not the life others expected of me.

2. I wish I hadn't worked so hard. (This was especially common for men.)

3. I wish I'd had the courage to express my emotions.

4. I wished I had stayed in touch with my friends.

5. I wish I had let myself be happier.

Regarding people's regret that they missed out on life by not letting themselves be happier, Bronnie wrote, "This is a surprisingly common one. Many did not [realize] until the end that happiness is a choice. They had stayed stuck in old patterns and habits. The so-called 'comfort' of familiarity overflowed into their emotions, as well as their physical lives. Fear of change had them pretending to others, and to [themselves], that they were content. When deep within, they longed to laugh properly and have silliness in their life again."[3]

Our days are numbered, no matter how old we are or what season of life we are in. All of us will die at some point—of that we can be certain (unless Jesus returns first). Although we can't change the past or get back the days we have wasted feeling unhappy and discontent with the lives God has given us, we can choose today to embrace a new attitude and outlook on life.

Abraham Lincoln once said, "And in the end, it's not the years in your life that count. It's the life in your years."[4] We get only one life to live. Isn't it time to start living it to the fullest by choosing to love the life God has given you, no matter what?

Are you ready to live the abundant life God intended for you and is waiting for you to embrace? Are you ready to make the absolute most of the time He has given you?

If you are excited about living life as if it's actually the priceless gift it is, don't wait another day. Start living life to the fullest by:

1. *Embracing contentment.* Recognize where discontentment resides in your heart and tackle it so it doesn't lay claim to your happiness another day.

2. *Recognizing your value.* Believe without a shadow of a doubt that you are a priceless treasure in God's eyes.

3. *Loving yourself.* Love yourself the way God loves you, and commit to trying to see yourself through His eyes instead of focusing only on what you see in the mirror or in the rearview mirror of your past.

4. *Accepting forgiveness.* Accept that God has forgiven you and remembers your sins no more. Believe you are clean and as white as snow from His point of view. Fully embrace His gift of unconditional forgiveness.

5. *Forgiving and forgetting.* Set yourself free from the prison of bitterness, hurt, and anger by letting go of the past and forgiving those who have hurt you. Remember the prisoner you are setting free is you.

6. *Conquering loneliness.* Don't let loneliness steal your joy, because you always have a Friend by your side. Commit to building that friendship with your Savior.

7. *Being a friend.* Pray for friends and expectantly and excitedly wait to see how God will fill your life with people. Always try to be the kind of friend you want to have.

8. *Laughing more.* Laugh a lot, smile frequently, and let joy permeate you from head to toe. Be the reason someone else smiles today.

9. *Turning complaining into praising.* Stop whining and complaining and start a habit of praising instead. Make every effort to look for reasons to praise God, especially when a wave of complaints begins to roll off your tongue.

10. *Stressing over the future no longer.* Don't worry about tomorrow or a hundred tomorrows down the road, because God already has things all planned out. Trust He has control of your future and it is a good, good plan because He is a good, good Father.

11. *Developing a thankful heart.* Fill your heart with so much thankfulness that ungratefulness has no room to grow.

12. *Being the answer to someone's prayer.* Be the hands and feet of Jesus. Try to do something nice for someone else every day. Being kind to others not only makes us feel good but also shifts our focus from problems to people.

13. *Reigniting your faith.* Ask God to ignite a flame in your heart, and spend time every day getting to know His story through Scripture. And start talking to Jesus as if He were standing right beside you all throughout the day. Because He is.

My friend, your happiness is up to you. Despite what has happened in the past and regardless of your circumstances and challenges right now, you are in control of how you choose to view the gift of life and how you live out that gift. Don't let another day go by without embracing joy. Implement the tips outlined in this book and bask in the fact that you are indeed alive. Be more determined than ever to truly live the life you were meant to live, because this is the only chance you have to live it. Give it your all. Make the most of every day.

Seize today! Let it be the first day of the rest of your very own joy-filled, dearly loved, amazing life.

Notes

CHAPTER 1

1. William Barclay, *The Gospel of John*, Daily Study Bible Series, rev. ed. (Philadelphia: Westminster, 1975), 2:60.

2. Joyce Meyer (@joycemeyer), Instagram video, October 16, 2017, www.instagram.com/p/BaUyYt-jMMs/?taken-by=joycemeyer.

CHAPTER 2

1. Shaun Dreisbach, "Shocking Body-Image News: 97% of Women Will Be Cruel to Their Bodies Today," *Glamour*, February 2, 2011, www.glamour.com/story/shocking-body-image-news-97-percent-of -women-will-be-cruel-to-their-bodies-today.

CHAPTER 3

1. "Our Research," Dove, accessed December 8, 2017, www.dove.com/us/en /stories/about-dove/our-research.html.

CHAPTER 4

1. Max Lucado, *Anxious for Nothing: Finding Calm in a Chaotic World* (Nashville: Thomas Nelson, 2017), 37.

2. Lucado, *Anxious for Nothing*, 41.

CHAPTER 5

1. "What Did Jesus Mean When He Said That We Should Forgive Others Seventy Times Seven?" GotQuestions.org, accessed December 8, 2017, www.gotquestions.org/seventy-times-seven.html.

2. "What Did Jesus Mean … ?" GotQuestions.org.

3. "Mark Twain Quotes," BrainyQuote.com, accessed December 8, 2017, www.brainyquote.com/quotes/quotes/m/marktwain109919.html.

CHAPTER 6

1. Mary Brophy Marcus, "Feeling Lonely? So Are a Lot of Other People, Survey Finds," CBS News, October 12, 2016, www.cbsnews.com/news /many-americans-are-lonely-survey-finds/.

2. Jennifer Caudle, quoted in Mary Brophy Marcus, "Feeling Lonely? So Are a Lot of Other People, Survey Finds," CBS News, October 12, 2016, www.cbsnews.com/news/many-americans-are-lonely-survey-finds/.

3. "The Top 20 Valuable Facebook Statistics—Updated November 2017," Zephoria Digital Marketing, November 1, 2017, https.//zephoria.com /top-15-valuable-facebook-statistics/.

4. Courtney Seiter, "The Secret Psychology of Facebook: Why We Like, Share, Comment and Keep Coming Back," Buffer, August 12, 2017, https://blog.bufferapp.com/psychology-of-facebook.

5. Dictionary.com, s.v. "friend," accessed December 9, 2017, www.dictionary.com /browse/friend?s=t.

6. Dictionary.com, s.v. "compassion," accessed December 9, 2017, www.dictionary.com/browse/compassion?s=t.

CHAPTER 8

1. University of Maryland Medical Center, "Laughter Helps Blood Vessels Function Better," *Science Daily*, March 16, 2005, www.sciencedaily.com /releases/2005/03/050310100458.htm.

2. John Haltiwanger, "Why Being Able to Laugh at Yourself Is Crucial to a Happy Life," Elite Daily, August 24, 2015, www.elitedaily.com/life/laugh-at -yourself-key-to-happiness/1186573.

3. Lawrence Robinson, Melinda Smith, and Jeanne Segal, "Laughter Is the Best Medicine: The Health Benefits of Humor and Laughter," HelpGuide.org, October 2017, www.helpguide.org/articles/emotional-health/laughter-is-the -best-medicine.htm.

4. "Charlie Chaplin," BrainyQuotes.com, Accessed February 23, 2018, www.brainyquote.com/quotes/charlie_chaplin_108932.

CHAPTER 10

1. Rosalind Ryan, "What Worrying Does to Your Health," DailyMail.com, accessed December 12, 2017, www.dailymail.co.uk/health/article-97853 /What-worrying-does-health.html#ixzz4hH1u4u4T.

2. Ryan, "What Worrying Does."

3. Harvard Health Publishing, "Anxiety and Physical Illness," *Harvard Women's Health Watch*, June 6, 2017, www.health.harvard.edu/staying-healthy/anxiety _and_physical_illness.

CHAPTER 11

1. Max Lucado, *Anxious for Nothing: Finding Calm in a Chaotic World* (Nashville: Thomas Nelson, 2017), 94–95.

2. Johnson Oatman Jr., "Count Your Blessings," 1897, public domain.

CHAPTER 12

1. Kimberly Yam, "10 Facts That Prove Helping Others Is a Key to Achieving Happiness," *Huffington Post*, March 20, 2015, www.huffingtonpost.com /2016/12/12/international-day-of-happiness-helping-_n_6905446.html.

2. Mark Snyder, quoted in Philip Moeller, "Why Helping Others Makes Us Happy," U.S. News & World Report, April 4, 2012, http://money.usnews .com/money/personal-finance/articles/2012/04/04/why-helping-others -makes-us-happy.

3. C. H. Spurgeon, "The Waterer Watered," *Metropolitan Tabernacle Pulpit* 11, no. 626 (1865): 229, www.spurgeon.org/resource-library/sermons/the-waterer -watered#flipbook/.

CHAPTER 13

1. John MacArthur, "The Lonely Ember," Inspirational Archive, accessed December 12, 2017, www.inspirationalarchive.com/texts/topics /evangelization/lonelyember.shtml.

CONCLUSION

1. Max Lucado, *Anxious for Nothing: Finding Calm in a Chaotic World* (Nashville: Thomas Nelson, 2017), 99.

2. Bronnie Ware, "The Top Five Regrets of the Dying: A Life Transformed by the Dearly Departing," Barnes and Noble, accessed December 13, 2017, www.barnesandnoble.com/w/the-top-five-regrets-of-the-dying-bronnie -ware/1105496434#/.

3. Bronnie Ware, "Top 5 Regrets of the Dying," *Huffington Post*, January 21, 2012, www.huffingtonpost.com/bronnie-ware/top-5-regrets-of-the-dyin_b _1220965.html.

4. Abraham Lincoln, Good Reads, accessed January 22, 2018, www.goodreads .com/quotes/5851097-and-in-the-end-it-s-not-the-years-in-your.

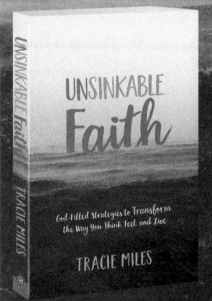